Preface

The survey and report were prepared by the Consumer and Community Development Research Section of the Federal Reserve Board's Division of Consumer and Community Affairs (DCCA).

DCCA directs consumer-related functions performed by the Board, including conducting research on consumer and community financial services, and community economic development opportunities and challenges.

DCCA staff members Sam Dodini, Alejandra Lopez-Fernandini, Ellen Merry, and Logan Thomas prepared this report. Valuable comments and feedback on the design of the survey and drafting of the report were provided by DCCA staff members Mario Arthur-Bentil, Anna Alvarez Boyd, Alexandra Brown, David Buchholz, Allen Fishbein, Arturo Gonzalez, Jeff Larrimore, Barbara Robles, and Jenny Schuetz, as well as by Federal Reserve System staff members Andrea Brachtesende, Marianne Crowe, Geoffrey Gerdes, Christopher Olson, and Elisa Tavilla.

Mention or display of a trademark, proprietary product, or firm in the report does not constitute an endorsement or criticism by the Federal Reserve System and does not imply approval to the exclusion of other suitable products or firms.

Contents

Executive Summary 1
    Key Findings 1

Introduction 3
    Survey Background 3
    Consumer Access to Mobile Phones 4
    Trends in the Utilization of Mobile Banking and Payments 5

Accessing Financial Services 7
    Mobile Banking 7
    Mobile Payments 15

Mobile Security and Privacy 21
    Perceptions of Safety and Risks 21
    Security Behaviors and Information Sharing 22

Use of Mobile Phones in Financial Decisionmaking 25
    Account Monitoring and Decisionmaking 25
    Shopping and Mobile Financial Management 26

Conclusion 27

Appendix A: Technical Appendix on Survey Methodology 29

Appendix B: Survey of Consumers' Use of Mobile Financial Services
2015—Questionnaire 33

Appendix C: Consumer Responses to Survey Questionnaire 61

Executive Summary

Mobile phones have increasingly become tools that consumers use for banking, payments, budgeting, and shopping. Given the rapid pace of change in the area of mobile finance, the Federal Reserve Board began conducting annual surveys of consumers' use of mobile financial services in 2011. The series examines trends in the adoption and use of mobile banking, payments, and shopping behavior and how the evolution of mobile financial services affects consumers' interaction with financial institutions.

This report presents findings from the latest survey, fielded in November 2015, which focused on consumers' use of mobile technology to access financial services and make financial decisions. Where applicable, the findings from the current survey are also compared with the findings from previous surveys. Topics include consumer access to bank services using mobile phones ("mobile banking"), consumer payment for goods and services using mobile phones ("mobile payments"), mobile security, and consumer financial management and shopping decisions facilitated by the use of mobile phones. Details about the survey, its methodology, and limitations can be found in the body of the report and in a methodological appendix. Survey data, as well as reports and data from previous years of the survey, are available on the Board's website at www.federalreserve.gov/communitydev/mobile_finance.htm.

Key Findings

Key findings of the 2015 survey include:

- **Mobile phones, particularly Internet-enabled smartphones, are in widespread use.**

  —Eighty-seven percent of the U.S. adult population has a mobile phone, the same as in 2014 and 2013.

  —Seventy-seven percent of mobile phones are smartphones (Internet-enabled), up from 71 percent in 2014 and 61 percent in 2013.

- **Adoption of mobile financial services continues to increase. A majority of consumers using these services cite convenience or getting a smartphone as their reason for adoption.**

  —Use of **mobile banking** continues to rise. Forty-three percent of all mobile phone owners with a bank account had used mobile banking in the 12 months prior to the survey, up from 39 percent in 2014 and 33 percent in 2013.

  —Fifty-three percent of smartphone owners with a bank account had used mobile banking in the 12 months prior to the survey, up from 52 percent a year earlier.

  —Consistent with previous years, the three most common mobile banking activities among mobile banking users were checking account balances or recent transactions (94 percent), transferring money between an individual's own accounts (58 percent), and receiving an alert (e.g., a text message, push notification, or e-mail) from their bank (56 percent).

  —Use of **mobile payments** continues to be less common than use of mobile banking. Twenty-four percent of all mobile phone owners reported having made a mobile payment in the 12 months prior to the survey.

  —Twenty-eight percent of smartphone users made a mobile payment in the 12 months prior to the survey.

  —The three most common mobile payment activities among mobile payments users with smartphones were paying bills through a mobile phone web browser or app (65 percent), purchasing a physical item or digital content remotely using a mobile phone (42 percent), and paying for something in a store using a mobile phone (33 percent).

- **Use of mobile financial services varies across demographic groups.**

  —Higher shares of younger adults, Hispanics, and non-Hispanic blacks reported using mobile banking and mobile payments than the overall survey averages. Smartphone ownership among those with mobile phones is higher for Hispanics than for non-Hispanic whites in this survey.

- **The main impediments to the adoption of mobile financial services cited by some consumers continue to be a preference for other methods of banking and making payments as well as concerns about security.**

  —Of those not using mobile banking, the primary reason respondents cited was a belief that their banking needs were being met without the use of mobile banking (88 percent).

  —The primary reason non-mobile-payment users gave for not using mobile payments was that they believe it is easier to pay with cash or credit/debit cards (80 percent).

  —Concern about the security of the technology was a common reason given for not using mobile banking or mobile payments (73 percent and 67 percent, respectively, of non-users).

- **Most consumers with bank accounts reported using a mix of online and offline channels to interact with their financial institution. For those who have adopted mobile banking, use of the mobile channel appears to complement their use of other banking channels.**

  —Among all respondents with bank accounts, the share using mobile banking is higher than the share using telephone banking but lower than the shares that have visited a branch, used an ATM, or used online banking in the last 12 months.

  —Among mobile banking users with smartphones, 54 percent cited the mobile channel as one of the three most important ways they interact with their bank, below the shares that cited online (65 percent) and ATM (62 percent), but above the share that cited a teller at a branch (51 percent).

- **The security and privacy of personal information remain common concerns for mobile phone users, and many smartphone users reported taking steps to guard against possible risks.**

  —Among those with a mobile phone, 42 percent think that people's personal information is "very unsafe" or "somewhat unsafe" when they use mobile banking, and an additional 15 percent "don't know" how safe these activities are.

  —The majority of smartphone users reported taking actions that can reduce harm in case of a security incident. The most common actions were installing updates (84 percent), password-protecting the phone (70 percent), and customizing privacy settings (58 percent).

  —Consumer awareness of security threats may influence behavior: 78 percent of smartphone users reported they do not download or install apps from sources outside their primary app store, and 76 percent reported they do not send or access sensitive data over public WiFi networks.

- **Consumers use their smartphones to inform financial decisions.**

  —Most mobile banking users who receive low-balance alerts from their bank reported taking some action in response, such as transferring money into the account with the low balance (43 percent), depositing money into the account (36 percent), or reducing their spending (32 percent).

  —Sixty-two percent of mobile banking users checked their account balance on their phone before making a large purchase in the 12 months prior to the survey. Half (50 percent) of them decided not to purchase an item as a result of their account balance or credit limit.

  —Forty-one percent of persons with smartphones used their phone to browse product reviews or get product information while shopping at a retail store, and 79 percent of them changed the item they purchased based on this information.

- **Mobile phones are prevalent among unbanked and underbanked consumers.**

  —Nine percent of consumers were unbanked at the time of the survey. Forty percent of the unbanked had access to a smartphone, 28 percent had access to a feature phone, and 32 percent lacked access to any type of mobile phone.

  —Twenty-two percent of consumers were underbanked, meaning they had a bank account and had used one or more alternative financial services (typically from a nonbank) within the past year. Seventy percent of the underbanked were smartphone owners, and 17 percent owned a feature phone.

  —Among the underbanked with mobile phones, 55 percent used mobile banking.

Introduction

In 2011, the Federal Reserve Board's Division of Consumer and Community Affairs conducted its first Survey of Consumers' Use of Mobile Financial Services (the "Mobile Survey"). Since that time, the adoption of mobile financial services has continued to increase, along with the range of services offered. As part of its ongoing efforts to monitor developments in the financial services arena and to gain insights into consumers' usage of, and attitudes toward, mobile financial services, the Board has continued to conduct the survey annually.[1] The fifth survey, conducted in November 2015, included a sample of respondents who had responded to both the 2013 and 2014 surveys, as well as a random sample of new respondents. The subsample of respondents who voluntarily completed both the 2014 and 2015 surveys allows for the analysis of changes in behavior over the past year among these individuals.

Survey Background

The original survey instrument and subsequent years of the survey were designed in consultation with a mobile financial services advisory group made up of key Federal Reserve System staff with relevant consumer research and payments backgrounds. The 2012, 2013, 2014, and 2015 survey samples were all composed of a mix of respondents to the previous year's survey and new survey respondents.

The 2015 survey was again administered by GfK, an online consumer research company, on behalf of the Board. The survey was conducted in English using a sample of adults ages 18 and over from KnowledgePanel®, a proprietary, probability-based web panel of more than 50,000 individuals from randomly sampled households; the sample was designed to be representative of the U.S. population. After

Table 1. Key survey response statistics: Main interview

Sample type	Number sampled for main survey	Qualified completes for analysis
2013–14 re-interviews	1,364	1,064
Fresh cases	2,324	1,446
Total primary sample	3,688	2,510

pretesting, the data collection for the survey began on November 4, 2015, and concluded on November 23, 2015.

As shown in table 1, e-mails were sent to 1,364 individuals who had responded to both the 2013 and 2014 surveys and 2,324 randomly selected individuals from the remaining members of KnowledgePanel®. The respondents completed the survey in approximately 12 minutes (median time). Of the 2,510 qualified respondents used for analysis in this report, 1,064 had responded to the 2013 and 2014 surveys, while 1,446 were new survey respondents drawn from the general population.[2] Further details on the survey methodology are included in appendix A.

As with any survey method, Internet panels can be subject to biases resulting from undercoverage or nonresponse and, in this case, potential underrepresentation of adults who may be uncomfortable with technology. Not everyone in the United States has access to the Internet, and there are demographic (income, education, age) and geographic (urban and rural) differences between those who do have readily available access and those who do not. These concerns about survey error for Internet surveys are addressed by GfK providing Internet access to respondents who do not have it in order to include the portion of the population that does not have Internet access in KnowledgePanel®, and by using

---

[1] See the "Consumers and Mobile Financial Services" reports series for previous years' survey findings. Results of the 2011, 2012, 2013, and 2014 surveys (published in March 2012, 2013, 2014, and 2015, respectively) are available at www.federalreserve.gov/communitydev/mobile_finance_publications.htm.

[2] The 2015 survey also included an oversample of non-Hispanic black and Hispanic respondents. For comparability with prior years of the survey, the oversample was not used in computing the results in this report; therefore, respondents from the oversample are not included in table 1.

sample weights to ensure that the Internet usage and key demographics of the sample population match the U.S. adult population. See appendix A for a more detailed discussion.

While these steps have been taken to make the survey results generalizable to the U.S. adult population, some caveats apply to interpretation of the results, particularly for subpopulations. This survey was conducted in English, and thus may not reflect the attitudes and behaviors of those in the U.S. population whose dominant language is not English. In addition, survey estimates about technology use may be affected by the mode of the survey, as a respondent's use of or views about technology could be correlated with the choice to participate in an Internet survey. Thus, these results may be more representative of those who would be willing and able to respond in English to an Internet survey. In particular instances, comparisons to outside data sources are included where they may shed some light on these issues.

The full survey questionnaire is presented in appendix B. In the cases in which questions were only asked of certain respondents conditional on their answer to a prior question, such information is also reported on the questionnaire. Responses to the survey questions are presented in appendix C in the order that the questions were asked of respondents. Tables of summary statistics for the respondent demographic characteristics by mobile phone usage are also included as tables C.64 to C.67. Beginning at table C.68, cross-tabulations are presented of consumers' use of mobile phones, mobile banking, and mobile payments by age, race, gender, education, and income.

The remaining sections of this report summarize key findings from the Federal Reserve Board's survey of consumers conducted by GfK, with a focus on how consumers use mobile phones to conduct their banking and make payments, as well as on how consumers perceive and protect the security of mobile transactions and manage their finances. All data were weighted to yield estimates for the U.S. adult population. The numbers cited in this report are derived from the Mobile Survey unless otherwise noted.

Consumer Access to Mobile Phones

As of November 2015, 87 percent of the U.S. population ages 18 and above owned or had regular access to a mobile phone. While the percent of the adult population with mobile phones has remained constant over the previous three years, an increasing proportion owns a smartphone: this survey's 77 percent smartphone ownership rate among those with mobile phones is a substantial increase over the 71 percent rate reported in 2014, 61 percent in 2013, 52 percent rate in 2012, and 44 percent rate in 2011.[3]

Rates of mobile phone usage remain high and consistent across demographic and socioeconomic groups. The prevalence of mobile phones demonstrates the extent to which they have become ingrained in modern culture. Mobile phone usage in the 2015 survey is higher among younger age groups: 91 percent for persons ages 18 to 44, 90 percent for persons 30 to 44, and 89 percent for persons 44 to 59. Mobile phone usage declines somewhat, to 81 percent for persons ages 60 and over. Smartphone adoption is similarly higher among younger generations, with the differences being more pronounced among age groups: 91 percent of those ages 18 to 29 and 88 percent of those ages 30 to 44 who own a mobile phone have a smartphone, while 72 percent of mobile phone owners ages 45 to 59 and 56 percent of mobile phone owners ages 60 and over have a smartphone.

Consistent with the results of prior years of this survey, results for the 2015 survey suggest that mobile phone ownership varies slightly by race and ethnicity, with non-Hispanic whites, Hispanics, and non-Hispanic blacks having ownership rates of 88 percent, 90 percent, and 83 percent, respectively. Adoption of smartphones in the Mobile Survey varies in a somewhat more pronounced way: 82 percent of Hispanic mobile phone users have a smartphone, compared to 74 percent of non-Hispanic whites and 76 percent of non-Hispanic blacks (table 2).[4] Among

---

[3] Throughout this report, percentages are calculated as a share of all those who were asked a question, including those who did not respond. Based on surveys conducted in 2015, the Pew Research Center reported that 92 percent of U.S. adults owned a mobile phone and 68 percent of U.S. adults had a smartphone. Expressed as a share of all adults for comparison, smartphone ownership for the 2015 Mobile Survey was 67 percent of U.S. adults. (See www.pewinternet.org/files/2015/10/PI_2015-10-29_device-ownership_FINAL.pdf.)

[4] Estimates from the 2015 Mobile Survey show larger differences between racial/ethnic groups in smartphone ownership rates than those found by the Pew Research Center. Results from a survey fielded by Pew in 2015 indicated that smartphone ownership rates were similar for the three largest groups: 66 percent for non-Hispanic whites, 68 percent for non-Hispanic blacks, and 64 percent for Hispanics. Expressed as a share of all adults for comparison, smartphone ownership rates for the 2015 Mobile Survey respondents used in this report were 65 percent for non-Hispanic whites, 63 percent for non-Hispanic blacks, and 74 percent for Hispanics. (See footnote 3 for a link to the

Table 2. Smartphone usage by race/ethnicity
Percent, except as noted

Race/ethnicity	Smartphone usage				
	2011	2012	2013	2014	2015
White, non-Hispanic	41	50	57	68	74
Black, non-Hispanic	47	54	63	66	76
Other, non-Hispanic	45	54	76	83	88
Hispanic	55	60	72	82	82
2+ races, non-Hispanic	43	59	64	65	79
Total	44	52	61	71	77
Number of respondents	2,002	2,291	2,341	2,603	2,244

Note: Among respondents with a mobile phone.

those with a mobile phone, smartphone ownership is also higher (88 percent) for the "Other, non-Hispanic" group, which includes respondents who report their race as Asian, American Indian or Alaskan Native, Hawaiian, or Pacific Islander.

Mobile phone and smartphone usage does vary with the level of household income. In households earning less than $25,000 per year, 76 percent of adults have a mobile phone of some type, and 58 percent of those with mobile phones have a smartphone. Use of both mobile phones and smartphones increases with income. Among those adults in households earning more than $100,000 per year, 96 percent have a mobile phone, and 86 percent of those with mobile phones have a smartphone.

Trends in the Utilization of Mobile Banking and Payments

Services that allow consumers to obtain financial account information and conduct transactions with their financial institution ("mobile banking") and that allow consumers to make payments, transfer money, or pay for goods and services ("mobile payments") have become increasingly prevalent. Over the past several years these services have become available at a broader range of institutions, and the types of services offered continue to evolve.

With increased dissemination of technology and a broadening array of options, consumer adoption of

mobile financial services has risen. In the 2011 survey, for instance, 22 percent of mobile phone users with bank accounts and 43 percent of smartphone users with bank accounts reported that they had used mobile banking in the previous 12 months.[5] These proportions have increased in each year of the survey. In the 2015 survey, the prevalence of mobile banking continued to increase, reaching 43 percent of mobile phone users with bank accounts and 53 percent of smartphone users with bank accounts (figure 1).

Use of mobile payments has also increased over time. In 2011, 12 percent of mobile phone users and 23 percent of smartphone users reported using mobile payments. By 2014, usage of mobile payments had increased to 22 percent for mobile phone users and to 28 percent for smartphone users. The steady increases in the adoption rate among all mobile phone users, but more gradual rise in the adoption rate among smartphone users, suggest that smartphone adoption substantially contributed to the increased use of mobile payments. The measure of mobile payments in the 2015 survey is not directly comparable to those from prior years due to a change in the definition of mobile payments in the most recent survey.[6] Despite this change, the new estimates appear similar to those from prior years, with 24 percent of mobile phone users and 28 percent of smartphone users reporting that they used mobile payments in 2015.

A continuing impediment to adoption of either mobile banking or mobile payments appears to be consumers' limited demand for them: many consumers said their needs were already being met without mobile banking or mobile payments, that they were comfortable with non-mobile options, and that they did not see a clear benefit from using either service. In addition, around one in five (21 percent) of those with mobile phones and bank accounts indicated they do not know if their bank or credit union offers mobile banking, which may be consistent with a lack

---

Pew report.) A variety of factors could contribute to differences in the measures, including survey coverage and question wording. Because the Mobile Survey was conducted in English, omission of the portion of the Hispanic population who may not feel comfortable responding in English may contribute to differences in measures of smartphone ownership for this group.

[5] Here, the figures for mobile banking in the 2011 survey are expressed as percentages of mobile phone users with bank accounts. These figures differ slightly from those published in the 2011 report, which were calculated as a percent of all mobile phone users. Similarly, other estimates in the text may differ from the figures presented in appendix C or from estimates published in earlier reports because a different subsample of the respondents was used for the calculation.

[6] The definition of mobile payments was revised for the 2015 Mobile Survey and is given on page 15 of this report. The definition of mobile payments used in the 2011 through 2014 surveys is included in footnote 13.

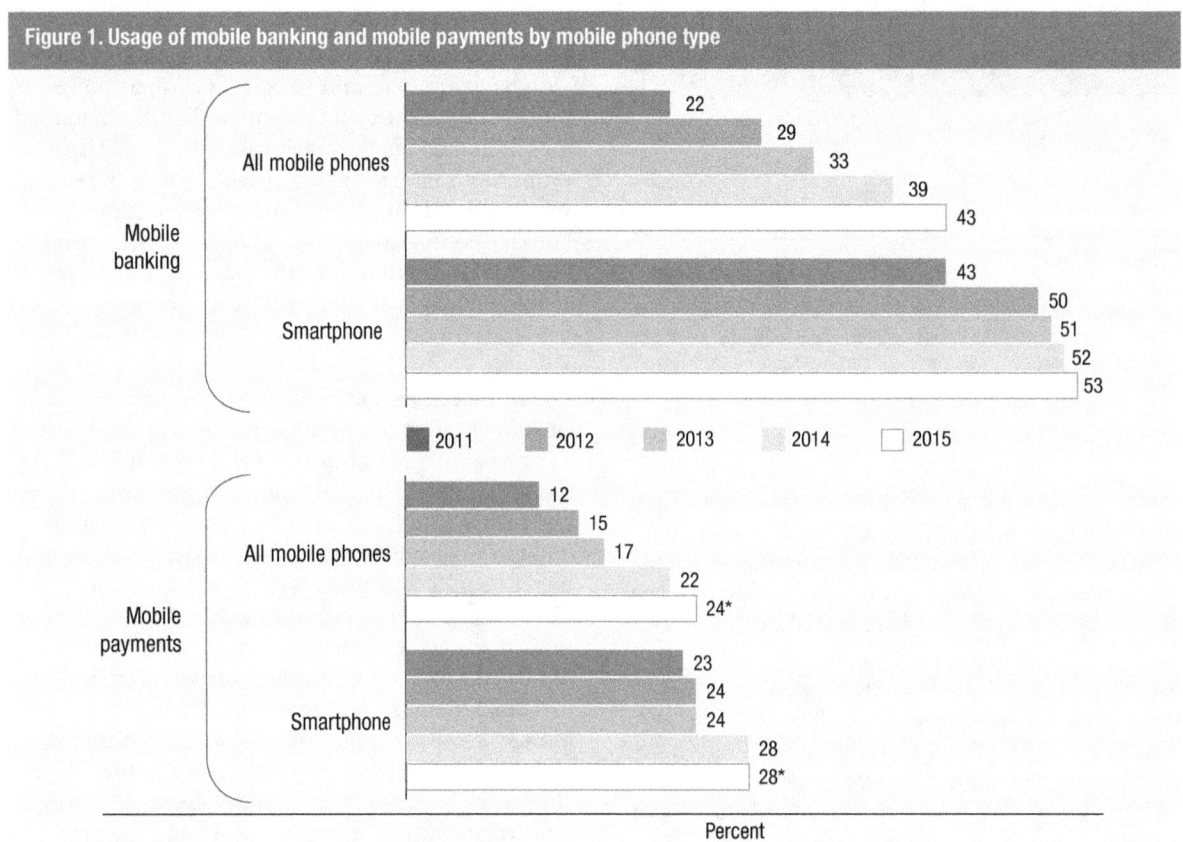

Figure 1. Usage of mobile banking and mobile payments by mobile phone type

Note: For mobile banking, among respondents with a mobile phone and bank account and respondents with a smartphone and bank account, respectively. For mobile payments, among respondents with a mobile phone and respondents with a smartphone, respectively.

* Not directly comparable to prior years due to question change in 2015.

of interest in these services among a portion of the population.

That said, the share who do not know if mobile banking is available from their bank has decreased from 28 percent in 2013, and 22 percent in 2014. The share that said their bank does not offer the service has shown less of a change—6 percent in 2013, 4 percent in 2014, and 5 percent in 2015. The decline in the share of "don't know" responses may suggest an increase in consumer awareness of mobile banking services over the last few years. As such, this might be an indication that financial institutions are increasing their marketing of existing mobile services as well as that more of them may be offering these services.

Concerns about the security of mobile banking and mobile payment technologies are also frequently cited as reasons why consumers chose not to adopt these technologies. These concerns are described in more detail later in this report.

Accessing Financial Services

Survey respondents were given a set of screening questions that asked if they had access to a bank account, the Internet, and a mobile phone. They were further asked about the various ways in which they access their financial accounts. Of the 91 percent of American consumers who have a checking, savings, or money market account, the majority use some form of technology to interact with their financial institution. (For a discussion of Internet access among Mobile Survey respondents, see box 1.)

As shown in figure 2, the most common way of interacting with a financial institution is in-person at a branch, with 84 percent of consumers who have a bank account reporting that they had visited a branch and spoken with a teller in the 12 months prior to the survey.[7] The second-most common means of access in the previous 12 months was using an automated teller machine (ATM) at 75 percent, followed by online banking at 71 percent. Thirty-eight percent of all consumers with bank accounts used mobile banking, up from 35 percent the previous year, while 30 percent used telephone banking.[8]

The share of respondents with bank accounts who use mobile banking has risen steadily since the 2011 Mobile Survey, surpassing the use of telephone banking.[9] Although use of online banking has risen modestly over this period, use of the bank channels other than mobile has been generally consistent. Because these measures capture use of a channel in the past year—not frequency of use or activities over time and across channels—they cannot adequately capture the possible substitution between mobile banking and other ways of interacting with a financial institution. Yet, they suggest that most consumers appear to be making use of multiple bank channels, and that for many who have adopted it, mobile banking is a complement to other ways of conducting banking business.

Mobile Banking

The Mobile Survey defines mobile banking as using "a mobile phone to access your bank or credit union account. This can be done either by accessing your bank or credit union's web page through the web browser on your mobile phone, via text messaging, or by using an app downloaded to your mobile phone." This section takes a more detailed look at mobile banking usage, focusing on mobile banking adoption, activities, and motivations for use.

Adoption Rates

The adoption of mobile banking has continued to increase in the past year. When asked about usage in the previous 12 months, 43 percent of mobile phone users with a bank account reported that they used mobile banking, a proportion that has been steadily climbing (figure 1). Mobile banking among smartphone users with a bank account is higher at 53 percent. The higher incidence of mobile banking adoption among smartphone users suggests that as smart-

---

[7] To measure the use of a bank branch in the 2015 Mobile Survey, respondents were asked the following question: "Have you visited a bank branch and spoken with a teller or a bank employee in the past 12 months? Please do not include visits where your only activity was using an ATM/Cash machine located at a branch." In prior years of the survey, the second sentence requesting that respondents exclude branch visits that only involved the use of an ATM was not included. Thus, the question from the 2015 survey may not be directly comparable to the measures from earlier surveys. This change in the question would likely reduce the measure of branch use in the last year, and thus could be a component of any year-over-year change.

[8] The relative prevalence and ranking of channel usage in the 2013 Mobile Survey is similar to results from the *2013 FDIC Survey of Unbanked and Underbanked Households*. See www.economicinclusion.gov/surveys/2013household/. However, the incidence of online banking and of households with Internet access are notably higher in the 2013 Mobile Survey than in the Federal Deposit Insurance Corporation (FDIC) survey. This may be due in part to differences in the survey methodology, as the FDIC survey is conducted by phone and in person while the Mobile Survey is conducted via an online panel.

[9] For an overview of the use of all five channels in previous Mobile Surveys, see figure 2 of the 2015 report, available at www.federalreserve.gov/econresdata/consumers-and-mobile-financial-services-report-201503.pdf.

Box 1. Internet Access among Mobile Survey Respondents

While smartphones are one of the more recent technological innovations transforming the ways consumers conduct their finances, laptop and desktop computers are still important avenues for interacting with financial institutions, searching for financial and other types of information, and purchasing goods and services. In addition to asking questions about mobile and smartphone ownership, the Mobile Survey includes questions about Internet connectivity on desktops, laptops, and tablets to gauge the range of options respondents may have for using technology for financial services.

For panelists who are recruited to join KnowledgePanel® but indicate they do not have Internet access, GfK provides basic Internet service and a web-accessible device so they can participate in surveys. To measure Internet access, the 2015 Mobile Survey asked respondents if they currently have regular access to the Internet at home that is not provided by GfK. To identify respondents who have Internet access other than what may be available through a smartphone, the question explicitly asked about use of the Internet on a computer (desktop, laptop) and a tablet (e.g., iPad). A similar question also asked about respondents' access to the Internet using a desktop, laptop, or tablet away from home—such as at school, work, a public library, etc.

As a group, 2015 Mobile Survey respondents have high rates of Internet connectivity apart from any basic service that may be provided by GfK. Fifty-four percent reported having access both at home and away from home. Another 28 percent have regular access at home only, and 7 percent have regular access only away from home. Ten percent of respondents did not report any access to the Internet on a desktop, laptop, or tablet. In sum, 82 percent of respondents had regular access to the Internet at home on a desktop, laptop, or tablet computer as of November 2015.[1]

[1] While the Mobile Survey's measures of Internet access are not directly comparable to other surveys, a general comparison may be useful for context. Estimates from the American Community Survey (ACS) show that 80 percent of U.S. households had Internet access at home in 2014, up from 79 percent in 2013. In addition to differences in the years the data were collected, survey coverage, question wording, and sampling unit (i.e., adult versus household) there are other differences in the measures.

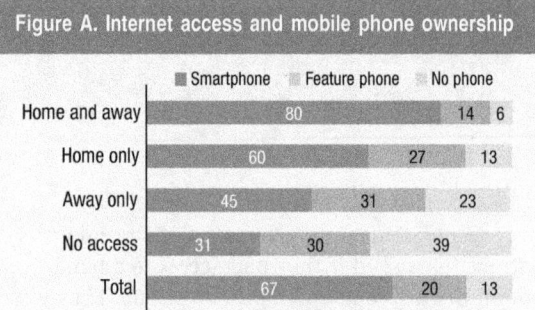

Figure A. Internet access and mobile phone ownership

	Smartphone	Feature phone	No phone
Home and away	80	14	6
Home only	60	27	13
Away only	45	31	23
No access	31	30	39
Total	67	20	13

Note: Among all respondents (n=2,510). Here and elsewhere in this report, totals may not add to 100 percent due to rounding and question non-response.

Respondents with Internet access at home are more likely to own mobile phones, particularly smartphones (figure A). Eighty percent of those who have access to the Internet on a desktop, laptop, or tablet both at home and away from home have smartphones, and 60 percent of those who have Internet access only at home have smartphones. Smartphone ownership rates among those respondents who do not have Internet access at home are lower, but still substantial: 45 percent for those who only have access to the Internet using a desktop, laptop, or tablet away from their home and 31 percent for those who do not have access at all.

Most survey respondents appear to have the option of interacting with their financial institutions through home Internet and/or smartphone connections, which can open access to a range of services, as well as product information. However, those who are reliant on Internet access away from home or who have no regular Internet access also are less likely to have smartphones or even basic feature phones and, thus, may face greater obstacles in obtaining financial services through online and mobile channels.

For example, unlike questions on the ACS, the Mobile Survey did not ask about the type of connection (i.e., broadband, mobile, or dialup). For discussion of the 2013 ACS estimate, see www.census.gov/history/pdf/2013comp-internet.pdf; the 2014 ACS figure is a Board staff calculation using estimates from the Census Bureau's American FactFinder tool.

---

phone adoption continues to increase, mobile banking usage may also increase.

A significant fraction of mobile banking users have only recently adopted the technology. Although the majority of mobile banking users reported that they started using it more than one year ago, 9 percent reported that they adopted mobile banking in the last six months, and 14 percent reported that they adopted mobile banking between six and twelve months ago. Among those consumers with mobile phones who do not currently use mobile banking,

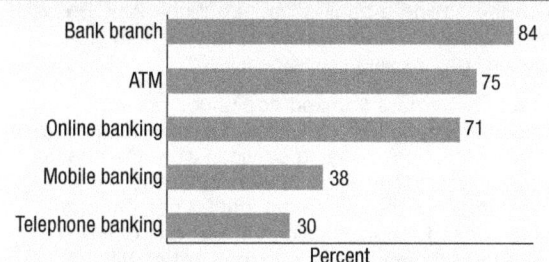

Figure 2. Usage of different means of accessing banking services

- Bank branch: 84
- ATM: 75
- Online banking: 71
- Mobile banking: 38
- Telephone banking: 30

Percent

Note: Among respondents with a bank account, regardless of mobile phone ownership or access to the Internet (n=2,373). For mobile banking, the percentage here differs from the incidence rates elsewhere in this report because the latter are computed for those with mobile phones and bank accounts.

Table 3. Use of mobile banking in past 12 months by age

Percent, except as noted

Age group	2011	2012	2013	2014	2015
18–29	45	54	63	60	67
30–44	29	37	43	54	58
45–59	12	21	25	32	34
60+	5	10	9	13	18
Total	22	29	33	39	43
Number of respondents	1,859	2,180	2,187	2,437	2,151

Note: Among those with a mobile phone and a bank account.

12 percent reported that they will "probably" or "definitely" use mobile banking in the following 12 months.

By examining responses from individuals who participated in both the 2014 and 2015 surveys, it is possible to compare reported mobile banking use from year to year. Among panel respondents with a mobile phone and a bank account in both surveys, most were consistent in their use (or lack of use) of mobile banking from year to year: 32 percent used mobile banking in both years, and 53 percent did not use mobile banking in either year. However, a small share reported a change between the surveys: 4 percent were mobile banking users in 2014, but reported that they had not used mobile banking in 2015, and 9 percent adopted mobile banking in 2015, implying a net increase in use among these panel respondents of approximately 5 percentage points.

Although previous surveys suggest that the reported adoption intentions of the respondents do not perfectly reflect subsequent behavior, there is an association between the planned use of mobile banking and subsequent adoption. Using the panel of respondents to both the 2014 and 2015 Mobile Surveys, it is possible to compare stated adoption intentions in 2014 to the reported use of mobile banking in 2015.

Of those consumers with a mobile phone and bank account in both years who reported in 2014 that they would "definitely" or "probably" adopt mobile banking in the following 12 months, 40 percent reported in the 2015 survey that they had used mobile banking during the previous 12 months. This is a higher proportion than those who said they did not expect their activity to change. Among those with a mobile phone and bank account in both years and indicated that they "probably will not" and "definitely will not" adopt mobile banking, 18 percent and 5 percent, respectively, reported in the 2015 survey that they had, in fact, used mobile banking in the previous 12 months.

For the group of respondents in the 2014 survey who believed they "definitely" or "probably" would use mobile banking in the coming year, the most notable difference between those who reported using mobile banking in the 2015 survey and those who did not was that the adopters were more likely to own a smartphone. Of this likely-to-adopt group, 41 percent with smartphones in 2015 used mobile banking, while 13 percent with feature phones used mobile banking.[10] In both the panel and cross-sectional data, smartphone users were more likely to engage in mobile banking than non-smartphone users.

In every year of the survey, older consumers have consistently been less likely to use mobile banking than younger consumers (table 3). For those with a mobile phone and a bank account, results from the 2015 survey indicate that mobile banking use is 67 percent for those in the 18-to-29 age range and 58 percent for those in the 30-to-44 age group. By comparison, only 18 percent of individuals ages 60 or older reported having used mobile banking. Usage has generally increased from year to year for all age groups. These differences by age reflect both the higher share of younger age groups who are smart-

---

[10] In this report, the term "feature phone" is used to refer to a mobile phone that is not a smartphone and has limited features aside from making calls. The Mobile Survey defines a smartphone as "a mobile phone with features that may enable it to access the web, send e-mails, download apps, and interact with computers. Smartphones include the iPhone, Blackberry, as well as Android and Windows Mobile powered devices." Respondents who indicated they had a mobile phone were provided with this definition of a smartphone and asked "Is your mobile phone a smartphone?" If they answered "No," they were assumed to have a feature phone.

Box 2. Banking Status and the Use of Mobile Banking and Payments

The relatively high prevalence of mobile phone and smartphone use among younger generations, minorities, and those with low levels of income—groups that are more likely to be unbanked or underbanked—makes mobile phones a potential platform for expanding financial access and inclusion.

In the 2015 Mobile Survey, 9 percent of respondents were unbanked, having reported that neither they nor their spouse have a checking, savings, or money market account.[1] Twenty-two percent of consumers were underbanked in 2015—defined here as having a bank account but also using an alternative financial service (typically from a nonbank provider), including a money order, check-cashing service, tax refund anticipation loan, pawn shop loan, payday loan, auto title loan, or a paycheck advance/deposit advance.[2] The remaining share of consumers who reported having a bank account but not using one of these alternative financial services (the "fully banked" group) was 69 percent.

Among both the unbanked and underbanked groups, transaction-based products such as money orders and check-cashing services were the primary types of alternative financial services used. Fifty-one percent of the unbanked and 92 percent of the underbanked reported using at least one of these two financial services, with money orders being more common. Usage of credit-based products—tax refund anticipation loans, pawn shop loans, payday loans, auto title loans, or a paycheck advance/deposit—is much lower, with 14 percent of the unbanked and 29 percent of the underbanked having reported utilizing at least one of these services. Fifty-six percent of the unbanked (and, by definition, 100 percent of the underbanked) used at least one type of alternative financial service.

Seventy percent of both the underbanked and fully banked groups reported owning a smartphone, whereas only 40 percent of the unbanked consumers do the same. Though unbanked respondents reported higher ownership rates of feature phones,

(continued on next page)

---

[1] In 2015, the wording of the bank account question was changed from that used in earlier years, so the measure of the unbanked is not comparable to the prior years. The 2015 question wording, which conforms to the language from the Board's Survey of Household Economics and Decisionmaking, was, "Do you ["and/or your spouse" / "and/or your partner"] currently have a checking, savings, or money market account?" In the 2013 and 2014 surveys, the question about bank accounts was, "Do you or does your spouse/partner currently have some type of bank or credit union account such as a checking, savings, or money market account?"

[2] Due to changes in the questions about the use of alternative financial services in different years of the Mobile Survey, the 2015 figure for underbanked households is not directly comparable to results from earlier years. Of particular note is the inclusion of paycheck advance/deposit advance as an alternative financial service, despite this type of service being available at some banks. Also, the list of alternative financial services included in this survey differ from those included in the FDIC's work on unbanked and underbanked groups, and thus comparability of underbanked figures across the two surveys must be approached with these differences in mind.

---

phone owners, as well as differences in the propensity to use mobile banking for those with a given type of phone. Among smartphone owners, this pattern of higher mobile banking adoption for the younger age groups is still very apparent.

Consistent with the data from previous surveys, minorities continue to be more likely to use mobile banking than non-Hispanic whites. In particular, Hispanic mobile phone users with bank accounts show a higher rate of use of mobile banking (56 percent) relative to mobile phone users with bank accounts overall (43 percent) (table 4).

Among those with a mobile phone and bank account, mobile banking use is more common for those with higher levels of education. Usage for those with a college degree or some college (47 percent) is greater than for those with a high school degree or less (35 percent). In addition, mobile banking usage for those mobile phone users with bank accounts with household incomes of $40,000 and above (45 percent) is greater than for those with incomes below $40,000 (38 percent). (For further discussion

Table 4. Use of mobile banking in the past 12 months by race/ethnicity
Percent, except as noted

Race/ethnicity	2011	2012	2013	2014	2015
White, non-Hispanic	19	26	30	34	37
Black, non-Hispanic	35	39	42	43	50
Other, non-Hispanic	23	31	35	48	55
Hispanic	29	36	45	53	56
2+ races, non-Hispanic	21	36	31	41	46
Total	22	29	33	39	43
Number of respondents	1,859	2,180	2,187	2,437	2,151

Note: Among those with a mobile phone and a bank account.

Box 2. Banking Status and the Use of Mobile Banking and Payments—continued

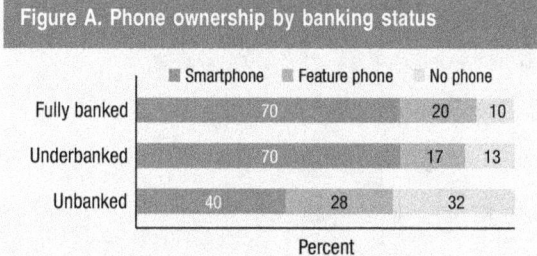

Figure A. Phone ownership by banking status

Note: Among respondents who were fully banked (n=1,941), underbanked (n=425), and unbanked (n=128).

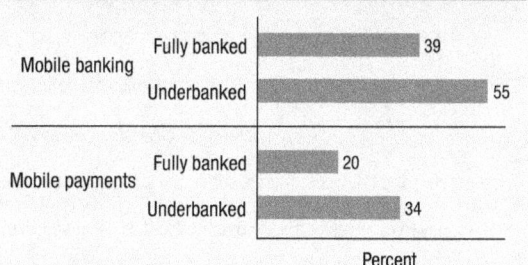

Figure B. Mobile banking and payments use by banking status

Note: Among respondents with a mobile phone who were fully banked (n=1,762) and underbanked (n=382).

the percentage of unbanked consumers with no phone (32 percent) was much higher than both the underbanked (13 percent) and fully banked (10 percent) groups (figure A).

Among the mobile phone owners, underbanked consumers were much more likely to report being either a mobile banking or mobile payments user than fully banked respondents (figure B). Fifty-five percent of underbanked consumers with mobile phones reported using mobile banking, and 34 percent reported using mobile payments. These figures compare with only 39 percent of the fully banked respondents with mobile phones using mobile banking and 20 percent using mobile payments.[3]

Some of the observed differences in the use of mobile financial services across these groups may be the result of differences in demographics. The underbanked have much higher percentages of younger adults, with 55 percent of the underbanked being between the ages of 18 and 44. This compares to only 42 percent of the fully banked group being in this same age range. Racial and ethnic differences are also notable across the different groups. Just 19 percent of the fully banked respondents are non-Hispanic black or Hispanic, whereas 45 percent of the underbanked group identified themselves as such.

---

[3] Due to the small sample size and inconsistencies in response patterns for mobile payments questions among the unbanked respondents, estimates of mobile payments use for the unbanked are not included.

---

about mobile banking use among the unbanked and underbanked, see box 2).

Common Mobile Banking Activities

Among those who reported using mobile banking in 2015, the most common mobile banking activity was checking financial account balances or transaction inquiries, with 94 percent of mobile banking users having performed this function in the 12 months prior to the survey (figure 3).[11] This was followed by transferring money between accounts, which was per-

formed by 58 percent of users. In addition, 56 percent of mobile banking users received an alert from their financial institution through a text message, push notification, or e-mail. Depositing a check to an account electronically using a mobile phone camera (known as remote deposit capture) and making an online bill payment from a bank account using a mobile phone were the next most common activities, done by 48 percent and 47 percent of mobile banking users, respectively. Mobile banking users appear to be using mobile applications to conduct their banking transactions, as 82 percent of mobile banking users have installed their bank's application on their phones.

Among all mobile banking users, the frequency of mobile banking use has been relatively consistent

---

[11] An alternative way of measuring mobile banking use would be to look at the share of respondents who report they have done one or more mobile banking activities in the last 12 months. For the 2015 Mobile Survey, 58 percent of those with a bank account and a mobile phone reported doing at least one mobile banking activity from the list in the survey. When limiting to only those with a bank account and smartphone, this number increases to 69 percent. This may suggest that the share of people using mobile banking may be somewhat higher than the measure obtained using the general definition.

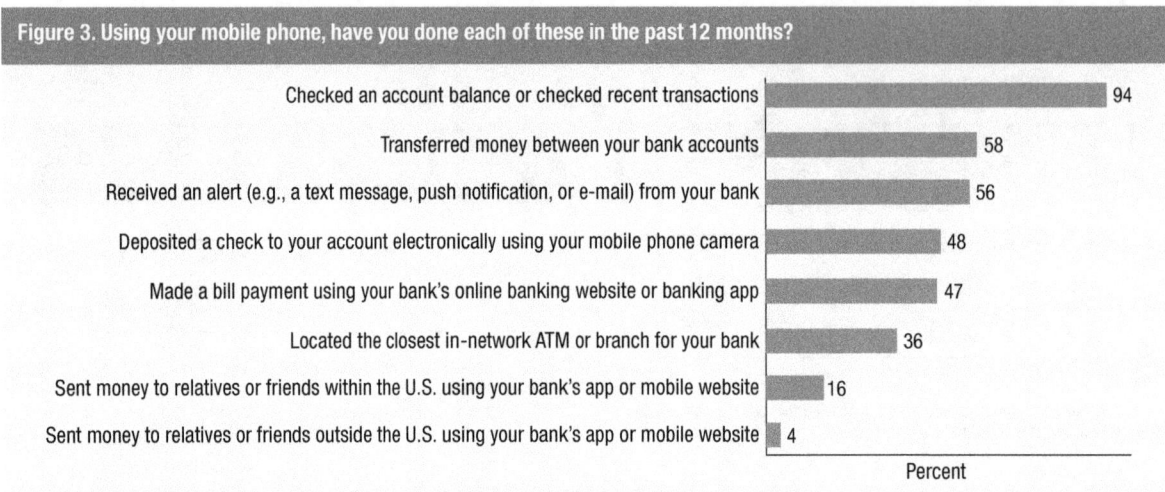

Figure 3. Using your mobile phone, have you done each of these in the past 12 months?

- Checked an account balance or checked recent transactions: 94
- Transferred money between your bank accounts: 58
- Received an alert (e.g., a text message, push notification, or e-mail) from your bank: 56
- Deposited a check to your account electronically using your mobile phone camera: 48
- Made a bill payment using your bank's online banking website or banking app: 47
- Located the closest in-network ATM or branch for your bank: 36
- Sent money to relatives or friends within the U.S. using your bank's app or mobile website: 16
- Sent money to relatives or friends outside the U.S. using your bank's app or mobile website: 4

Percent

Note: Among respondents with a mobile phone and bank account who used mobile banking in the past 12 months (n=801).

over the past several years. Among those who used mobile banking in the month prior to the survey, the median reported usage was five times per month in 2015 and 2014, and four times per month in 2013. Median usage for those with bank accounts who reported using mobile banking was also five times per month in both 2011 and 2012.

Among mobile banking users, there is variation in how frequently people use mobile banking services, and what types of activities they engage in. A relatively small share of mobile banking users (9 percent) indicated that they had used mobile banking in the previous year but had not used it in the previous month.

These low-intensity users have a lower likelihood of engaging in all types of mobile banking activities, relative to mobile banking users overall. Like all mobile banking users, the most common task for low-intensity users is checking account balances or recent transactions (71 percent). Forty-four percent of the low-intensity users have their bank's mobile banking app on their phone—a sizeable share, but far lower than the 82 percent of all mobile banking users who have installed their bank's app in their mobile phone. A greater proportion of low-intensity mobile banking users are non-Hispanic white (68 percent) compared to all mobile banking users (58 percent). Further, a greater proportion of low-intensity mobile banking users are ages 45 or older (43 percent), relative to all mobile banking users (32 percent).

In contrast, high-intensity users—defined here as mobile banking users who have conducted mobile banking tasks more than 10 times during the month prior to the 2015 survey—tend to conduct all mobile banking tasks at the same or higher rates than the larger group of users.[12] In particular, high-intensity users reported transferring money between their own accounts, making bill payments using their bank's mobile website or banking app, receiving alerts, and locating an ATM or branch for their bank at much higher rates than all mobile banking users. High-intensity users include greater shares of younger and Hispanic mobile banking users, relative to all mobile banking users.

Reasons for Using—or Not Using—Mobile Banking

Convenience continues to be the most common reason consumers give for adopting mobile banking. Indeed, 39 percent of consumers indicated that the convenience was the main reason they started using mobile banking (figure 4). Twenty-six percent of consumers said getting a smartphone was the main reason for using mobile banking. A further 19 percent of consumers indicated that the timing of their adoption of mobile banking was driven by their bank starting to offer the service.

Among those consumers with mobile phones and bank accounts who do not currently use mobile

---

[12] For the purposes of this report, "high-intensity" users are identified as those respondents who have used mobile banking within the year prior to the 2015 survey and have used mobile banking more frequently than 75 percent of all mobile banking users, which corresponds to a frequency greater than 10 times in the month prior to the 2015 survey. Based on this definition, high-intensity users represent 30 percent of mobile banking users in the 2015 survey.

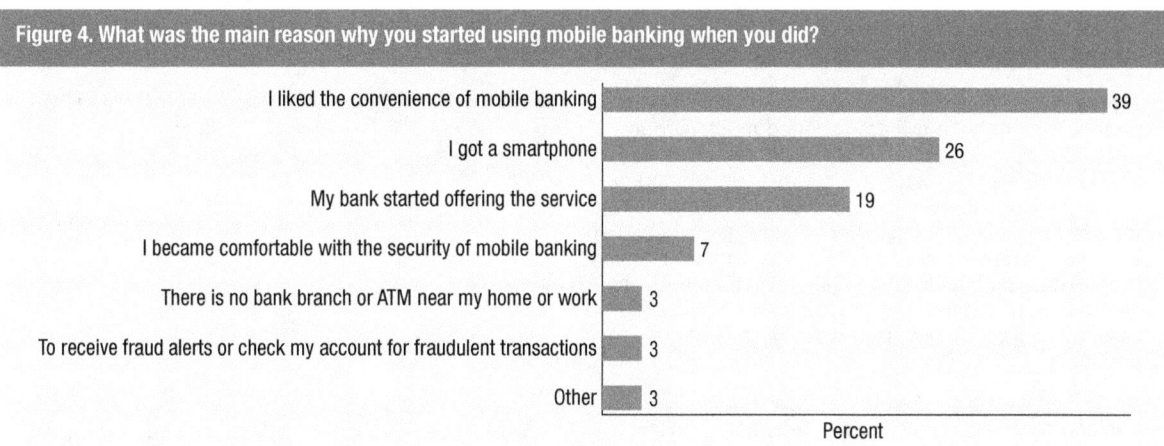

Figure 4. What was the main reason why you started using mobile banking when you did?

- I liked the convenience of mobile banking: 39
- I got a smartphone: 26
- My bank started offering the service: 19
- I became comfortable with the security of mobile banking: 7
- There is no bank branch or ATM near my home or work: 3
- To receive fraud alerts or check my account for fraudulent transactions: 3
- Other: 3

Percent

Note: Among respondents with a mobile phone and bank account who used mobile banking in the past 12 months (n=801).

banking, several reasons for not using the service predominated—namely, they believe that their banking needs are being met without mobile banking (88 percent), they do not see any reason to use mobile banking (78 percent), and they are concerned about security (73 percent). The small size of the mobile phone screen was cited by 43 percent of consumers as the reason they do not use mobile banking. This was followed by a lack of trust in the technology (40 percent) and not having a smartphone (27 percent) as reasons for not using mobile banking. Less commonly cited reasons included the difficulty associated

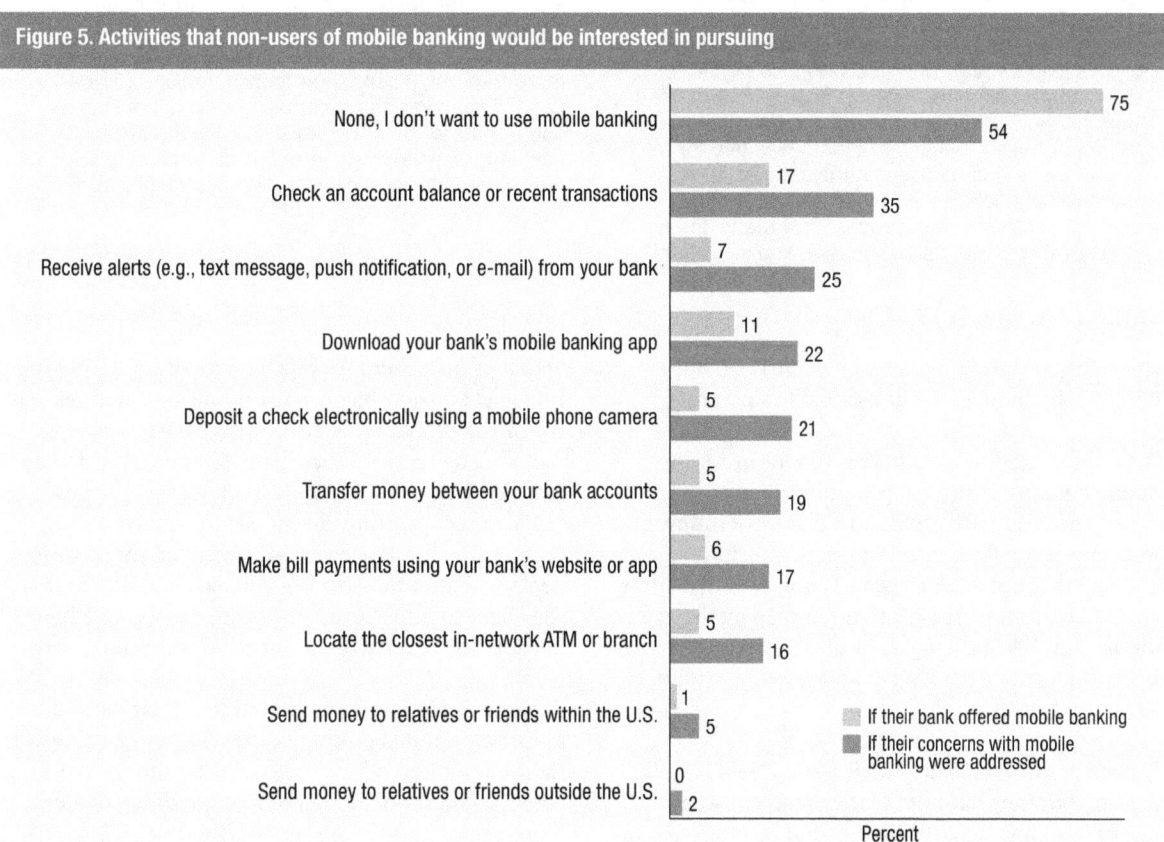

Figure 5. Activities that non-users of mobile banking would be interested in pursuing

Activity	If their bank offered mobile banking	If their concerns with mobile banking were addressed
None, I don't want to use mobile banking	75	54
Check an account balance or recent transactions	17	35
Receive alerts (e.g., text message, push notification, or e-mail) from your bank	7	25
Download your bank's mobile banking app	11	22
Deposit a check electronically using a mobile phone camera	5	21
Transfer money between your bank accounts	5	19
Make bill payments using your bank's website or app	6	17
Locate the closest in-network ATM or branch	5	16
Send money to relatives or friends within the U.S.	1	5
Send money to relatives or friends outside the U.S.	0	2

Percent

Note: Among those with a mobile phone and bank account who did not use mobile banking in the past 12 months, for those whose bank offered mobile banking (n = 819) and whose bank did not (n=536).

Box 3. Channel Use among Smartphone Users

Among those with bank accounts and mobile phones, smartphone owners reported much higher rates of mobile banking usage (53 percent) than feature phone users (7 percent). However, even among those smartphone owners who utilize mobile banking services, many still need or want to use other banking channels. For example, a visit to an ATM or branch may be necessary to withdraw cash, and visiting a branch or talking with a customer service representative may be preferred ways of resolving problems.

Respondents were asked about their use of five banking channels (branch, ATM, telephone, online, and mobile), and the answers provide a fuller picture of how smartphone users interact with their bank or credit union. In the prior 12 months, 83 percent of smartphone owners with bank accounts visited a branch and spoke with a teller, 82 percent used an ATM, 82 percent used online banking, 53 percent used mobile banking, and 29 percent used telephone banking (table A).

Among those smartphone owners who used each of these channels in the past year, most had used that same channel in the past month, with the incidence of use in the past month being the highest for the users of the online, mobile, and ATM channels (96 percent, 89 percent, and 87 percent, respectively). The frequency of use was also higher for these three channels. Among those who had used each of the channels in the past month, the median number of uses in the past month was five for each of the online and mobile channels, three for ATM, and two for each of the branch and telephone channels. These responses suggest that many smartphone owners use online, mobile, and ATM banking

Table A. Channel access among smartphone users
Percent, except as noted

Channel	Past 12 months*	Past month**	Top 3 ways interact with bank*
Branch	83	78	62
ATM	82	87	62
Telephone	29	67	16
Online	82	96	59
Mobile	53	89	31

* Among respondents with a smartphone and a bank account (n=1,622).
** Among respondents with a smartphone and a bank account who have used that channel in the past 12 months (n varies, depending on channel).

quite consistently for their banking needs, and the branch and telephone banking channels on a more periodic basis.

In a separate question, respondents were asked to select the most important ways they interact with their bank or credit union. Responses were limited to three channel selections. Among smartphone owners, a teller at a branch (62 percent), ATM (62 percent), and online banking (59 percent) were more frequently cited than mobile banking (31 percent). The lower share choosing mobile banking is due in part to the lower level of adoption of mobile banking, relative to some of the other channels. Among smartphone owners who use mobile banking, 54 percent cited mobile as one of their top three

(continued on next page)

---

with using mobile banking (18 percent) and not doing the banking in the household (15 percent).

The reasons respondents have given for not using mobile banking have been generally consistent among the 2013, 2014, and 2015 surveys. However, over time, a smaller share of respondents have reported that not having a smartphone (44 percent in 2013, 32 percent in 2014) was a reason why they had not used mobile banking. (For more information on the use of various banking channels by smartphone users, see box 3.)

Consumers who indicated their bank offers mobile banking but they did not use it were asked what mobile banking activities they would be interested in performing if their concerns were addressed. Their top responses included several of the most common activities of current mobile banking users. Checking financial account balances or recent transactions was the most commonly cited (35 percent), followed by receiving alerts from their bank (25 percent), downloading their bank's mobile banking app (22 percent), and depositing checks electronically (21 percent) (figure 5). However, 54 percent of these respondents who do not use mobile banking indicated that they had no interest in performing any mobile banking activities even if their concerns were addressed.

Separately, those who indicated that their bank did not offer mobile banking or that they did not know if their bank offered it were asked what mobile banking activities they would be interested in doing if their bank began to offer the service (figure 5). Checking financial account balances or recent transactions topped the list (17 percent), followed by downloading

Box 3. Channel Use among Smartphone Users—continued

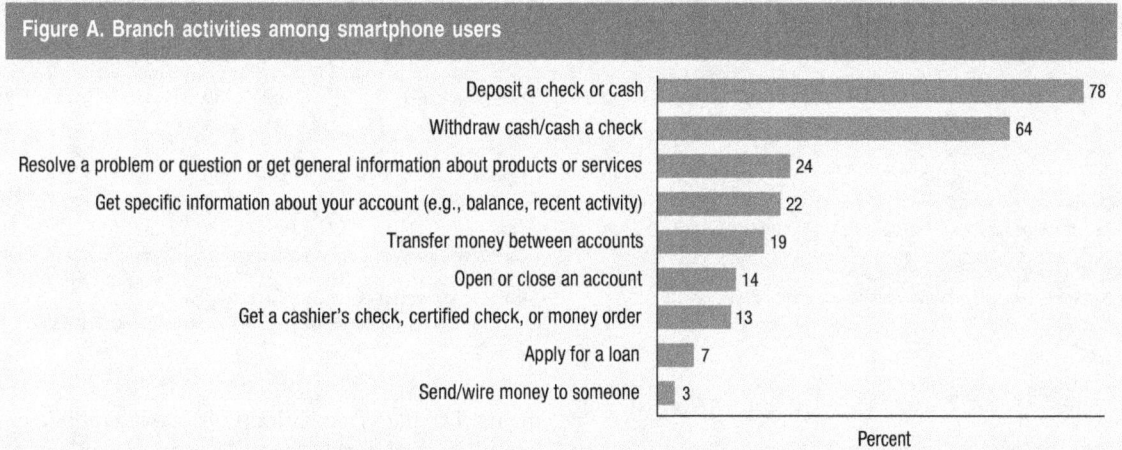

Figure A. Branch activities among smartphone users

Note: Among respondents with a smartphone and bank account who have visited a bank branch in the past 12 months (n=1,376).

channels—below the shares that cited online (65 percent) and ATM (62 percent), but above the share that cited a teller at a branch (51 percent). Those mobile banking users who said that mobile is one of their top three channels tend to be younger and have higher levels of education than those mobile banking users who do not.

The types of activities conducted using different channels are likely one driver of the frequency of channel use. As noted in this report, the most common activities among mobile banking users were checking financial account balances or transaction inquiries, transferring money between accounts, and receiving alerts. Among smartphone owners with bank accounts who reported visiting a branch in the past 12 months, the two most frequently cited reasons for visiting a branch were depositing (78 percent) or withdrawing (64 percent) a check or cash (figure A). Resolving a problem or getting general information about products or services (24 percent), obtaining specific information about an account (22 percent), and transferring money between accounts (19 percent) were also cited by many respondents.

Taken together, these estimates indicate that while smartphone owners are utilizing the mobile platform to interact with their bank or financial institution, they also rely on online banking and have maintained more traditional connections via the branch and ATM channels.

their bank's mobile banking app (11 percent). While other mobile banking activities did garner interest from smaller shares of this group, the dominant response was that most had no interest in performing any mobile banking activities (75 percent).

Mobile Payments

For purposes of this survey, mobile payments are defined as "purchases, bill payments, charitable donations, payments to another person, or any other payments made using a mobile phone. This includes using your phone to pay for something in a store as well as payments made through an app, a mobile web browser or a text message."[13] This section takes a more detailed look at mobile payment usage, focusing on mobile payment adoption, activities, and motivations for use.

---

[13] The definition of mobile payments was revised for the 2015 Mobile Survey. For the 2011 through 2014 surveys, the following definition of mobile payments was provided to respondents: "Mobile payments are purchases, bill payments, charitable donations, payments to another person, or any other payments made using a mobile phone. You can do this either by accessing a web page through the web browser on your mobile device, by sending a text message (SMS), or by using a downloadable application on your mobile device. The amount of the payment may be applied to your phone bill (for example, Red Cross text message donation), charged to your credit card, or withdrawn directly from your bank account."

Table 5. Use of mobile payments in the past 12 months by age
Percent, except as noted

Age group	2011	2012	2013	2014	2015*
18–29	20	26	28	34	30
30–44	16	18	21	31	32
45–59	8	9	13	16	20
60+	5	8	7	7	13
Total	12	15	17	22	24
Number of respondents	2,002	2,291	2,341	2,603	2,244

Note: Among respondents with a mobile phone.
* Not directly comparable to prior years due to question change in 2015.

Table 6. Use of mobile payments in the past 12 months by race/ethnicity
Percent, except as noted

Race/ethnicity	2011	2012	2013	2014	2015*
White, non-Hispanic	10	13	12	17	19
Black, non-Hispanic	14	18	34	34	32
Other, non-Hispanic	15	17	16	24	45
Hispanic	20	18	26	32	29
2+ races, non-Hispanic	9	13	31	23	26
Total	12	15	17	22	24
Number of respondents	2,002	2,291	2,341	2,603	2,244

Note: Among respondents with a mobile phone.
* Not directly comparable to prior years due to question change in 2015.

Adoption Rates

Mobile payments continue to be less common than mobile banking. Based on the responses to the broad definition of mobile payments listed above, 24 percent of those with access to a mobile phone reported that they made a mobile payment in the 12 months prior to the survey. Rates of mobile payment usage are somewhat higher among smartphone users: 28 percent of smartphone users reported having made a mobile payment in the previous 12 months.

Of current mobile payments users, 10 percent had started using mobile payments in the prior six months, while 16 percent began using mobile payments six to twelve months prior to the survey. An additional 20 percent reported that they started using mobile payments in the prior one to two years, and 30 percent reported that they began using mobile payments more than two years prior to the survey. Twenty-one percent of users are unable to recall when they began using mobile payments.

Younger consumers are more likely to make mobile payments (table 5). Of those with a mobile phone in 2015, 30 percent of individuals ages 18 to 29 and 32 percent of individuals ages 30 to 44 had made mobile payments. By comparison, 13 percent of those ages 60 or over reported making mobile payments. This pattern of use by age has been evident across all five years of the survey.

Among those owning a mobile phone, minorities are more likely to make mobile payments (table 6). In 2014, 32 percent of non-Hispanic blacks with mobile phones and 29 percent of Hispanics with mobile phones had made mobile payments, while 19 percent of non-Hispanic whites reported making mobile payments. The pattern of minorities making mobile payments at a higher rate than white, non-Hispanic consumers has persisted over time in the Mobile Survey.

There is no clear relationship between mobile payment usage and income or education level among those who own a mobile phone.

Common Mobile Payment Activities

Focusing only on those smartphone owners who reported that they had made a mobile payment in the prior 12 months, the most common mobile payment activity was paying bills (65 percent), followed by purchasing a physical item or digital content remotely using a mobile phone web browser or app (42 percent) (figure 6). The next most common activities reported by mobile payments users were paying for something in a store (33 percent) and sending money to friends or relatives within the United States (25 percent). Less common activities were paying for parking, a taxi, car service, or public transit using a mobile phone (20 percent); making a donation or payment by text message (12 percent); and sending money to relatives or friends outside the United States (5 percent).[14]

Although using a mobile phone to pay for a retail purchase at the point-of-sale (POS) is less common than paying bills or purchasing physical items or digi-

---

[14] An alternative way of measuring mobile payments use would be to look at the share of respondents who report they have done one or more mobile payments activities in the last 12 months. For the 2015 Mobile Survey, 30 percent of those with a mobile phone and 38 percent of those with a smartphone reported doing at least one mobile payment activity from the list in the survey. This may suggest that the share of people using mobile payments may be somewhat higher than the measure obtained using the general definition.

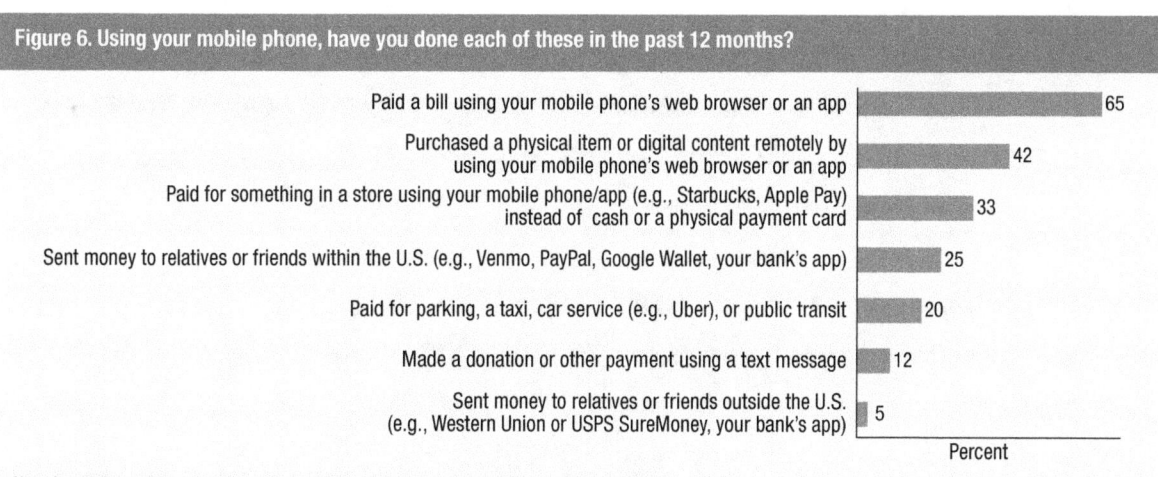

Figure 6. Using your mobile phone, have you done each of these in the past 12 months?

- Paid a bill using your mobile phone's web browser or an app: 65
- Purchased a physical item or digital content remotely by using your mobile phone's web browser or an app: 42
- Paid for something in a store using your mobile phone/app (e.g., Starbucks, Apple Pay) instead of cash or a physical payment card: 33
- Sent money to relatives or friends within the U.S. (e.g., Venmo, PayPal, Google Wallet, your bank's app): 25
- Paid for parking, a taxi, car service (e.g., Uber), or public transit: 20
- Made a donation or other payment using a text message: 12
- Sent money to relatives or friends outside the U.S. (e.g., Western Union or USPS SureMoney, your bank's app): 5

Percent

Note: Among those with a smartphone who used mobile payments in the past 12 months (n=406).

tal content remotely with a phone, POS mobile payments are no longer rare. Developments in technology, the entrance of new market participants, and increased familiarity with mobile payments may be contributing to this trend. As noted earlier, in 2015, 33 percent of all mobile payments users with smartphones had paid for something in a store using their mobile phone instead of cash or a payment card in the 12 months prior to the survey. Among those mobile payments users with smartphones who made POS mobile payments, 73 percent had made a POS payment in the preceding month, and over a third had made more than two such payments.

Mobile payments are most commonly funded using debit cards (56 percent), credit cards (48 percent), directly from a bank account (36 percent), or from an account at a non-financial institution such as PayPal (16 percent). Only 9 percent of mobile payments users reported that they used a prepaid debit card, and 3 percent had the charge directly applied to their phone bill. The type of payment used to fund the mobile purchase has implications for the consumer protections that the payer is afforded on the transaction, as different payment sources are covered by different consumer regulations and regulatory agencies.[15]

Among all mobile payments users, the median reported frequency of using mobile payments was two times in the month prior to the survey. As with mobile banking, there is variation among mobile payments users in how frequently they use the service and in types of activities. Twenty-five percent of mobile payments users reported they had used mobile payments in the last 12 months but not in the month prior to the survey. Like the overall group of mobile payments users, the most common mobile payment activity reported by these low-intensity users is paying bills (30 percent).

Twenty-one percent of mobile payments users reported that they had used mobile payments more than four times in the month prior to the survey.[16] Compared to all mobile payments users, these high intensity mobile payments users had higher rates of engaging in all mobile payments activities and tended to engage in a few mobile payment activities at much higher rates. In particular, relative to all mobile payments users, high-intensity users more frequently reported that they paid their bills online through a mobile web browser or app and purchased a physical item or digital content remotely using a mobile phone web browser or app.

Reasons for Using—or Not Using—Mobile Payments

Convenience is the most common reason given by consumers who have adopted mobile payment activity (45 percent). Getting a smartphone is the second

---

[15] For further details on how existing consumer regulations relate to the various methods for making mobile payments, see Stephanie Martin, "Statement before the Committee on Financial Services Subcommittee on Financial Institutions and Consumer Credit U.S. House of Representatives" (Washington: Federal Reserve Board, June 2012), www.federalreserve.gov/newsevents/testimony/martin20120629a.pdf.

[16] For the purposes of this report, "high-intensity" mobile payments users are identified as those respondents who have used mobile payments within the year prior to the 2015 survey and have used mobile payments more frequently than 75 percent of all mobile payments users, which corresponds to a frequency greater than four times in the month prior to the 2015 survey.

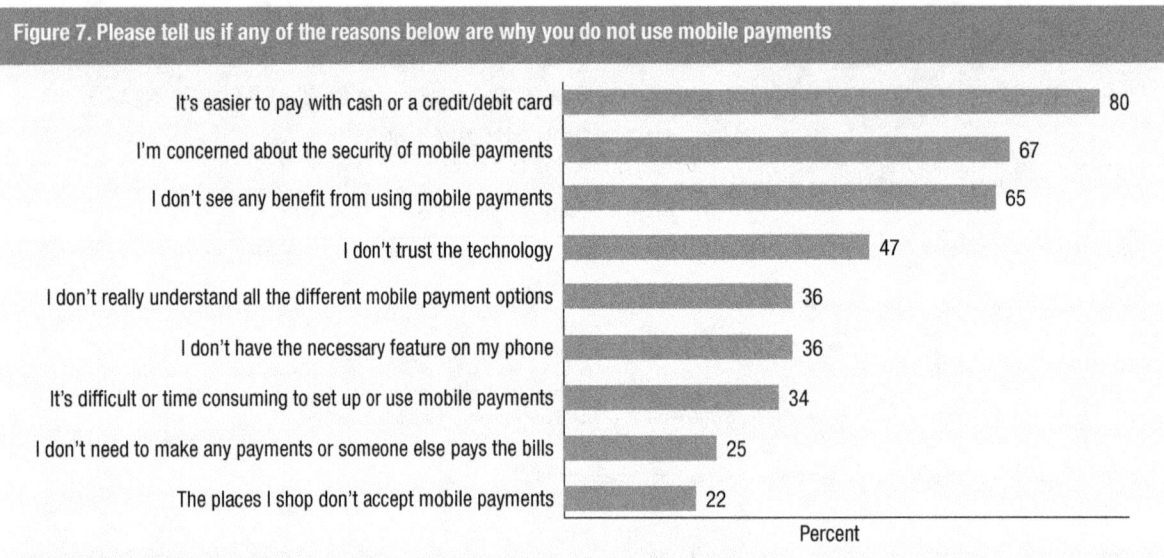

Figure 7. Please tell us if any of the reasons below are why you do not use mobile payments

- It's easier to pay with cash or a credit/debit card — 80
- I'm concerned about the security of mobile payments — 67
- I don't see any benefit from using mobile payments — 65
- I don't trust the technology — 47
- I don't really understand all the different mobile payment options — 36
- I don't have the necessary feature on my phone — 36
- It's difficult or time consuming to set up or use mobile payments — 34
- I don't need to make any payments or someone else pays the bills — 25
- The places I shop don't accept mobile payments — 22

Percent

Note: Among respondents with mobile phones who did not use mobile payments in the past 12 months (n=1,802).

most common reason people started using mobile payments (20 percent). Fourteen percent of users said the ability to make mobile payments becoming available to them was the main reason, while 7 percent indicated that they began using mobile payments because they became comfortable with the security.

Among those who said they do not use mobile payments, the most common reason for not adopting the technology is that they prefer to use other means of making payments: 80 percent reported that it is easier to pay with other methods (figure 7). Sixty-seven percent cited security concerns, and a similar proportion (65 percent) did not see a benefit to using mobile payments.

The reasons respondents have given for not using mobile payments have been generally consistent between the 2013, 2014, and 2015 surveys. However, over time, a smaller share of respondents have reported that not having the necessary features on their phone (46 percent in 2013, 37 percent in 2014) and the places they shop not accepting mobile payments (27 percent in 2013, 23 percent in 2014) were reasons why they had not used mobile payments.

When consumers who do not use mobile payments were asked to indicate all the mobile payment activities they would have an interest in using if their concerns were addressed, 74 percent indicated that they simply had no interest in using mobile payments even if their concerns were addressed (figure 8). This is similar to the responses regarding mobile banking, indicating that some consumers simply have no interest in utilizing the new technology under any circumstances.

Of the potential activities of interest to others, using a mobile phone to pay for purchases at a store was the most commonly cited (17 percent). Three other mobile payment activities appealed to a sizeable share (12 percent for each activity): paying for parking, a taxi, car service, or public transit; paying a bill; and purchasing a physical item or digital content remotely using a mobile phone.

When those with a smartphone who did not report making POS payments were asked if they plan to use their mobile phone to make a payment in a store in the next 12 months, 5 percent said they "definitely will" and 15 percent said they "probably will." The majority of smartphone users said that they "probably will not" (50 percent) or "definitely will not" (30 percent) use their phone to make an in-store payment.

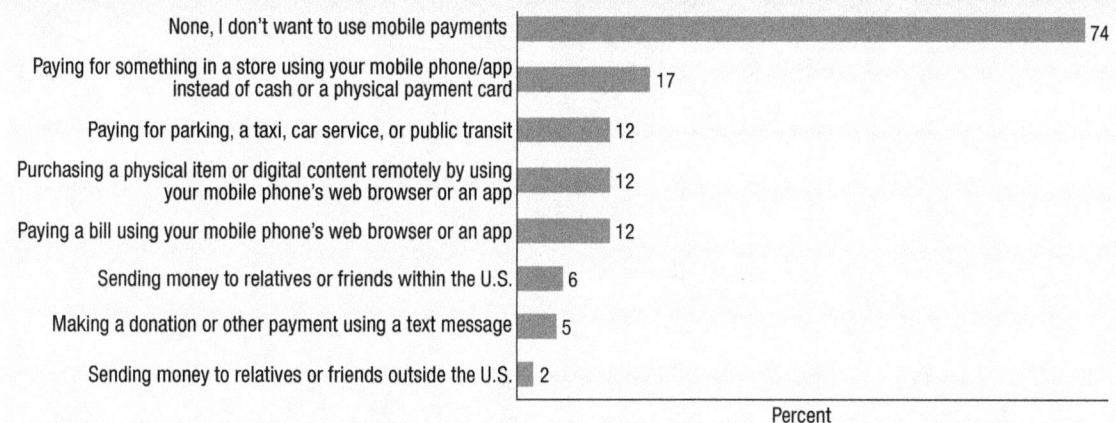

Figure 8. Assuming that the reason(s) why you do not currently use mobile payments was addressed, would you be interested in doing any of the following activities with your mobile phone?

Note: Among respondents with mobile phones who did not use mobile payments in the past 12 months (n=1,802).

Mobile Security and Privacy

Perceptions of Safety and Risks

One of the main reservations consumers have with adopting mobile banking and mobile payments is concern about the security of the technology. Despite the increasing prevalence of mobile banking and mobile payments, a significant share of consumers believe the technology to be unsafe or do not know how safe it is.

Among all mobile phone users, 24 percent believed that people's personal information is "somewhat unsafe" when using mobile banking, and 18 percent believed that it is "very unsafe." A further 15 percent of mobile phone users simply did not know how safe it is to use mobile banking. Only 8 percent said it was "very safe" to use mobile banking.

While the share of respondents with concerns is similar to previous years, there is a slight shift toward more reassurance about people's safety with mobile banking among consumers over the course of the last three Mobile Surveys: in 2015, 43 percent of mobile phone users said they believe people's personal information is either "very safe" or "somewhat safe," an increase from 40 percent in 2014 and 38 percent in 2013 (table 7).

When mobile phone users were asked how safe they believe people's personal financial information is

Table 7. How safe do you believe people's personal information is when they use mobile banking?
Percent, except as noted

Response	2013	2014	2015
Very safe	6	7	8
Somewhat safe	32	34	35
Somewhat unsafe	25	25	24
Very unsafe	18	19	18
Don't know	17	15	15
Number of respondents	2,341	2,603	2,244

Note: Among respondents with a mobile phone.

Table 8. How safe do you believe people's personal information is when they use a mobile phone to pay for a purchase at a store?
Percent, except as noted

Response	2013	2014	2015
Very safe	4	5	6
Somewhat safe	30	30	32
Somewhat unsafe	27	28	27
Very unsafe	19	21	19
Don't know	18	15	15
Number of respondents	2,341	2,603	2,244

Note: Among respondents with a mobile phone.

when they use a mobile phone to pay for a purchase at a store, 27 percent said it was "somewhat unsafe" and 19 percent said it was "very unsafe." As with mobile banking, there exists significant uncertainty about the security of POS mobile payments, with 15 percent saying they "don't know" whether people's personal financial information is safe when making such a payment. The share of consumers who said that POS mobile payments are "very safe" was only 6 percent, while 32 percent said that it is "somewhat safe."

As with mobile banking, there has been a slight shift over time in perceptions of the safety of using a mobile phone to pay for a purchase in a store. In 2015, 38 percent of respondents said that using a mobile phone to pay for a purchase in a store is either "very safe" or "somewhat safe," an increase from 35 percent in 2014, and 33 percent in 2013 (table 8).[17]

Mobile banking users have more confidence and less uncertainty about the security of mobile banking transactions, compared to non-users. Among mobile phone owners with bank accounts, the majority of mobile banking users rated mobile banking as "very

---

[17] Due to rounding differences, the figure in the text for 2013 differs slightly from the sum of elements of table 8 for that year.

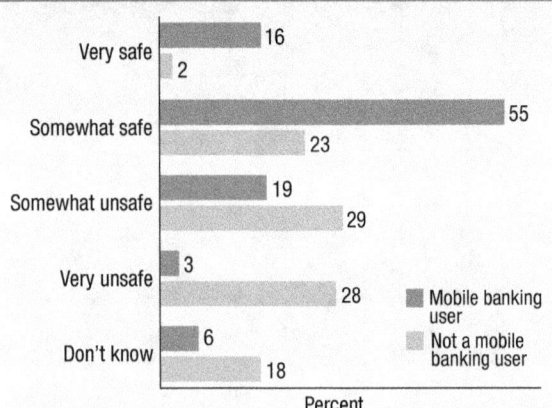

Figure 9. How safe do you believe people's personal information is when they use mobile banking?

Note: Among respondents with a mobile phone and bank account, for those who used mobile banking (n=801) and those who did not use mobile banking (n=1,343) in the past 12 months.

safe" (16 percent) or "somewhat safe" (55 percent) in maintaining their personal information. Only 6 percent of mobile banking users indicated that they "don't know" how safe mobile banking is at protecting their personal information. In contrast, non-users were less likely to rate the overall security of mobile banking as "very safe" (2 percent) or "somewhat safe" (23 percent). Eighteen percent of non-users indicated that they "don't know" how safe it is to use mobile banking (figure 9).

Mobile phone owners were asked which one aspect of security would cause them the most concern about using a mobile phone for financial transactions such as mobile banking or paying for a purchase in a store (figure 10).[18] Some reported fears of the phone being hacked or data interception (25 percent), lost or stolen phones (13 percent), and companies not providing sufficient security to protect mobile transactions (7 percent). While other specific concerns were noted by smaller numbers of respondents, the most common response was that they were concerned with all of those security risks occurring (37 percent). Only 8 percent of those with mobile phones indicated that they had no concerns about the security of mobile financial transactions.

Security Behaviors and Information Sharing

Consumers appear to be cognizant of the need to protect the personal information stored on, and transmitted with, their phones. Seventy percent of smartphone owners reported that they password-protect their phone—in line with the 69 percent in 2014, and up from 61 percent in 2013 and 54 percent in 2012.[19]

---

[18] For the first time, the 2015 Mobile Survey asked all mobile phone users about their security concerns, regardless of whether the respondent had used their phone for mobile banking or mobile payments in the past year. In the past, similar questions were only asked of those who said that security concerns were a reason they had not adopted mobile banking or mobile payments.

[19] At least one major mobile phone operating system has changed its default settings to require users to set a password unless they

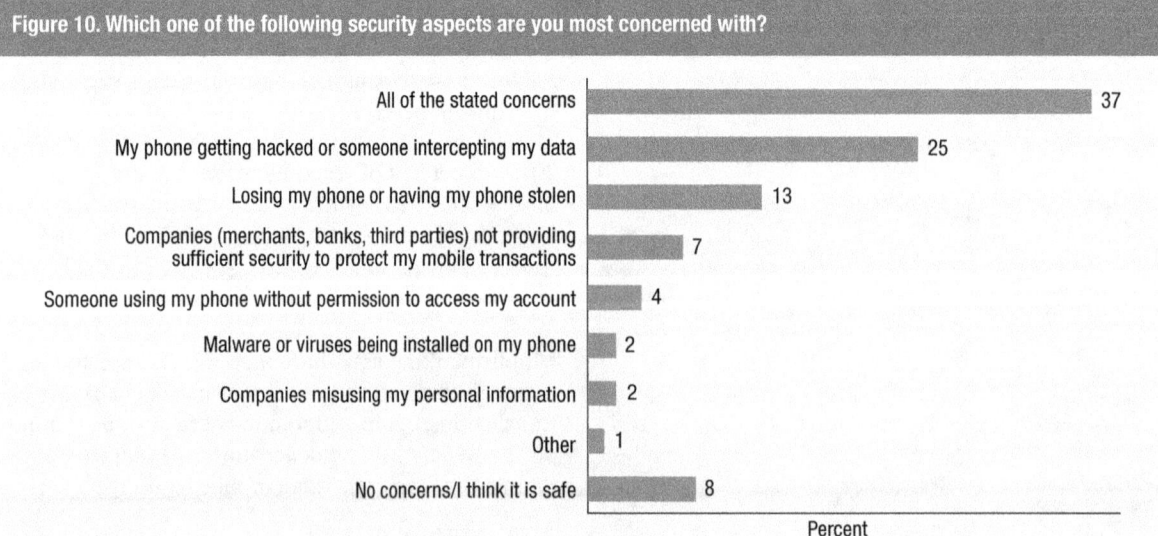

Figure 10. Which one of the following security aspects are you most concerned with?

Note: Among respondents with a mobile phone (n=2,244).

In the 2015 Mobile Survey, smartphone owners were also asked a new question about other specific actions they may have taken with their smartphone that affect mobile security and privacy.[20] Eighty-four percent of smartphone owners installed or updated their mobile operating system or apps, and 58 percent customized privacy settings, such as restricting which apps can track their location. Forty-three percent changed the password on their phone or apps, and 39 percent password-protected apps that store sensitive data. Thirty-three percent used anti-malware software or apps or other means to protect their smartphone, and 33 percent used an app or service that allows them to locate, remotely access, erase, or disable the phone in cases of loss or theft.

For the two actions on the list that increase mobile security risks, responses from smartphone owners also suggested that they avoid potential risks: 78 percent did not download or install apps from sources outside the primary app store for their phone, and 76 percent did not send or access sensitive data over public WiFi networks.

The sizable share of smartphone users who have restricted privacy settings on their phone is consistent with the preferences this group expressed about sharing their location. Smartphone users were asked about their level of agreement with the statement "I am willing to allow my mobile phone to provide my location to companies I shop with regularly so that they can offer me discounts, promotions, or services

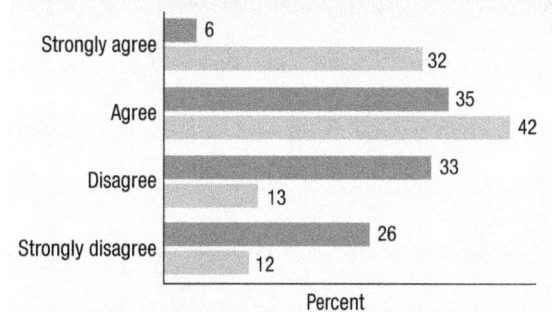

Figure 11. Willingness to provide information using mobile phone

■ I am willing to allow my mobile phone to provide my location to companies I shop with regularly so that they can offer me discounts, promotions, or services based on where I am.

■ I am willing to answer security questions or provide additional information to my bank or credit union when I log into mobile banking so my bank can enhance the security of my mobile transaction.

Note: Among smartphone users (n=1,680).

based on where I am." There appears to be significant discomfort with providing one's location to companies, as 33 percent indicated that they "disagree" and 26 percent "strongly disagree" (figure 11).

When smartphone owners were asked about their level of agreement with the statement "I am willing to answer security questions or provide additional information to my bank or credit union when I log into mobile banking so that my bank can enhance the security of my mobile transaction," the response pattern was quite different. In this case, the majority agreed—32 percent indicated they "strongly agree" and 42 percent that they "agree." Thirteen percent said they "disagree" and 12 percent indicated they "strongly disagree."

---

opt out. This change in default setting could also increase the incidence of password protection.

[20] Questions about password protection and specific actions taken to enhance security were only posed to respondents with smartphones. Feature phone users are likely to use their phones for a more limited set of tasks, and may not have given as much thought to potential security risks given the more limited functionality of these types of phones. Also, feature phones may not have password protection or other security options.

Use of Mobile Phones in Financial Decisionmaking

Account Monitoring and Decisionmaking

As the use of mobile financial services increases, mobile phones are increasingly becoming tools for managing personal finances and controlling spending. For example, 62 percent of mobile banking users with smartphones reported using their mobile phone to check account balances or available credit before making a large purchase in the 12 months prior to the survey. Of those who checked their balance or available credit, 50 percent reported that they decided not to buy an item because of the amount of money in their bank account or the amount of available credit.

Many consumers have near-constant access to their mobile phones, and these results illustrate that these devices have the potential to provide "just-in-time information" that can influence consumer financial behavior.

In addition, mobile phones can provide readily accessible and timely prompts that may help consumers make different, informed, and perhaps smarter, financial decisions. The actions consumers take in response to the receipt of text message or e-mail notices from their financial institutions demonstrate some of the potential effects of this technology for encouraging consumers to engage in informed financial behaviors that may prove to have beneficial outcomes.

More than half (52 percent) of mobile banking users receive alerts from their bank, and low-balance alerts are received by the majority of this group (figure 12). Most mobile banking users who received a low-balance alert from their bank reported taking some action in response: transferring money into the

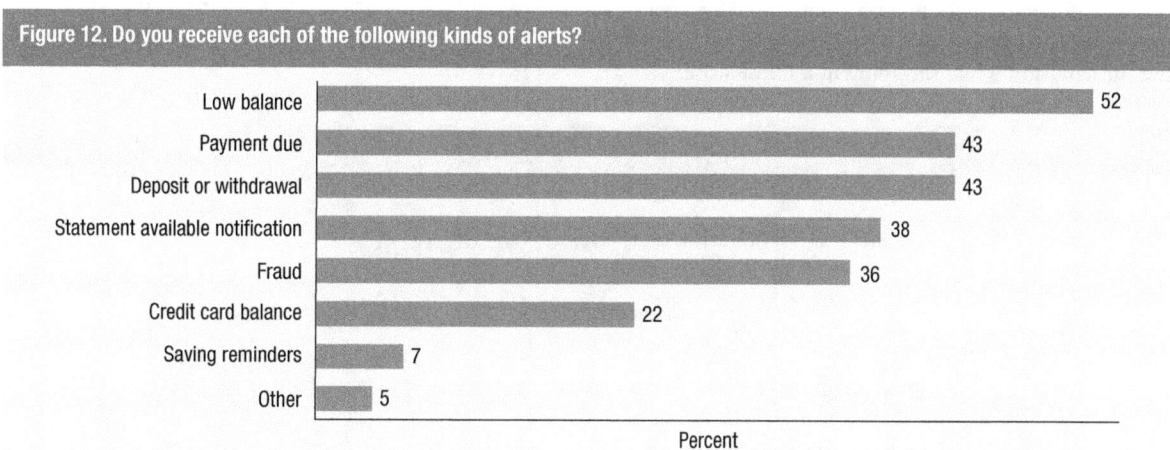

Figure 12. Do you receive each of the following kinds of alerts?

Alert type	Percent
Low balance	52
Payment due	43
Deposit or withdrawal	43
Statement available notification	38
Fraud	36
Credit card balance	22
Saving reminders	7
Other	5

Note: Among respondents with a mobile phone and bank account who used mobile banking in the past 12 months and who receive alerts (n=437). Respondents may receive alerts from their financial institution via push notification, text message, or e-mail.

account with the low balance (43 percent), depositing additional money into the account (36 percent), or reducing their spending (32 percent). Twenty-one percent reported taking no action in response to receiving a low-balance alert.

Shopping and Mobile Financial Management

In-Store Product Research and Price Comparison

Consumers are using their mobile phones to comparison shop and obtain product information while in retail stores. The prevalence of smartphones with barcode scanning software and Internet access has altered consumer behavior in the retail environment. With this technology, consumers can compare prices across retailers while in a store or online, or locate an item that is out of stock.

Among smartphone owners, 45 percent said that they have used their mobile phone to comparison shop on the Internet while at a retail store, and 28 percent have used a barcode scanning application for price comparisons, a 5 percentage point decline from the 2014 survey. Consumers are also using their smartphones to obtain product information: 29 percent have scanned a Quick Response (QR) code in a newspaper, magazine, or billboard advertisement to obtain information about a product, and 41 percent have used their phone to get product reviews or product information while shopping at a retail store.

Many consumers who use their smartphone to comparison shop reported that they altered their decisions as a result: 69 percent who have comparison shopped in a store reported that they changed where they made a purchase after comparing prices, and 79 percent reported that they changed what they purchased as a result of reading product reviews on their smartphone while at a retail store.

Interest in Mobile Services

Mobile financial management is an area with potential for consumer benefit. While many mobile phone users already use their mobile phones for tasks such as tracking purchases and expenses and comparing prices when shopping, mobile phone users expressed interest in expanding the range of functions they could perform with their phones.

Consumers were asked to select the types of activity they would be interested in performing with their mobile phones, assuming the functions were made available to them (figure 13). Some consumers appear to be open to greater use of their phones as a tool to get the best prices in their shopping activities: 23 percent expressed an interest in using their mobile phones to compare prices while shopping; 25 percent indicated that they would like to receive and manage discount offers and coupons; and 22 percent would like to receive location-based offers. Mobile phone users also expressed an interest in using their phones to store gift cards or track loyalty/reward points (22 percent) and to manage their personal finances (14 percent).

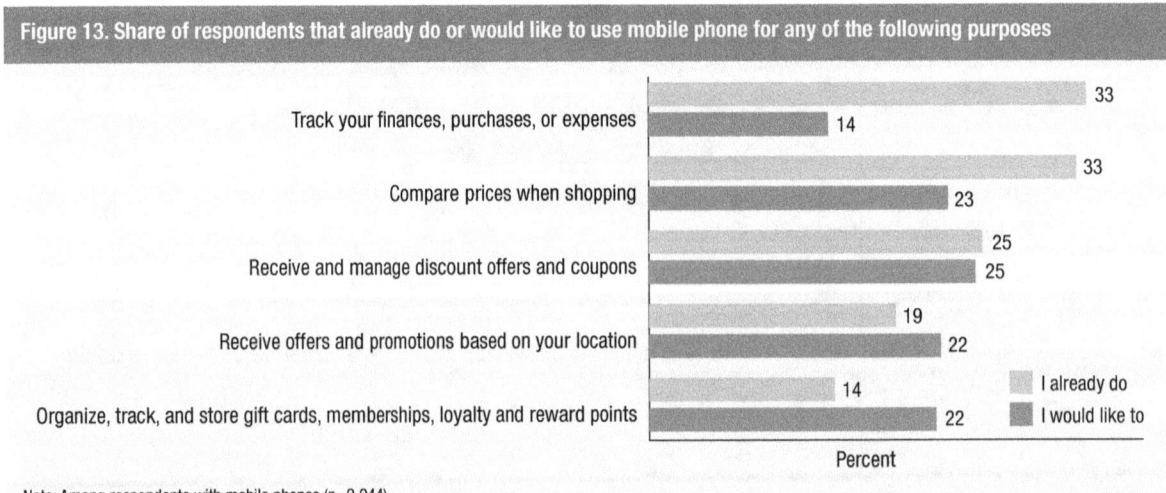

Figure 13. Share of respondents that already do or would like to use mobile phone for any of the following purposes

Note: Among respondents with mobile phones (n=2,244).

Conclusion

The use of mobile banking continued to rise in the past year and appears likely to continue to increase as more consumers use smartphones or recognize the convenience of this service, and as more financial institutions offer mobile banking. The most common tasks for mobile banking users continued to be checking account balances, transferring funds, and receiving alerts. The use of mobile payments, broadly defined, was lower than the use of mobile banking. As in the previous survey, the most common mobile payments activities were paying bills through a mobile phone or web browser, purchasing a physical item or digital content remotely using a mobile phone, and paying for something in a store using a mobile phone.

The main factors limiting consumer adoption of mobile banking and payments were a preference for using other methods for banking or making payments and security concerns. In terms of the value proposition to consumers, the significant number of mobile users who reported an interest in using their phones to receive discounts, coupons, and promotions or to track rewards and loyalty points suggests that tying these services to a mobile payment service may increase the attractiveness of mobile phones as a means of payment.

As smartphones become more common and more versatile, they can play an increasingly large role in the interactions between consumers and financial service providers, retailers, and other businesses. The near-constant presence of mobile phones in consumers' lives also makes them a potentially useful tool for the delivery of just-in-time financial information or as an aid in decisionmaking. Given the prevalence of mobile phones—particularly smartphones—among minorities, low-income individuals, and younger persons, mobile technology has the potential to empower consumers and expand access to financial services for underserved populations. However, consumers will need to understand and weigh the perceived benefits and potential risks to their security and privacy presented by the use of this evolving technology.

Appendix A: Technical Appendix on Survey Methodology

In order to create a nationally representative probability-based sample, GfK's KnowledgePanel® has selected respondents based on both random digit dialing and address-based sampling (ABS). Since 2009, new respondents have been recruited using ABS. To recruit respondents, GfK sends out mailings to a random selection of residential postal addresses. Out of 100 mailings, approximately 14 households respond to GfK and express an interest in joining the panel. Of those who express an interest in joining, around 64 percent complete the process and become members of the panel.[21] If the person contacted is interested in participating but indicates he or she does not have a computer or Internet access, GfK provides him or her with a web-enabled device and basic Internet service. Panel respondents are continuously lost to attrition and added to replenish the panel, so the recruitment rate and enrollment rate may vary over time.

For the 2015 Mobile Survey, a total of 5,461 KnowledgePanel® members received e-mail invitations to complete the survey, including both the primary sample and an oversample of non-Hispanic black and Hispanic respondents. The primary sample included 1,364 out of the 1,489 KnowledgePanel® respondents who participated in the Mobile Surveys for both 2013 and 2014 and who were still a part of KnowledgePanel® and could be assigned to the 2015 survey. (See table 1 in main text.) From this group of re-interviewed respondents, 1,071 people (excluding breakoffs) responded to the e-mail request to participate and completed the survey, yielding a final stage completion rate of 78.5 percent. The recruitment rate for the re-interviewed respondents, reported by GfK, was 15.9 percent and the profile rate was 63.4 percent, for a cumulative response rate for this sample of 7.9 percent. The primary sample also included an additional 2,324 randomly selected KnowledgePanel® respondents who did not participate in the previous Mobile Survey. From this sample of fresh cases, a total of 1,458 people (excluding breakoffs) responded to the e-mail request to participate and completed the survey, yielding a final stage completion rate of 62.7 percent. The recruitment rate for the fresh sample, reported by GfK, was 12.8 percent and the profile rate was 64.3 percent, for a cumulative response rate of 5.2 percent. From the 2,529 primary sample respondents who completed the survey, 9 were excluded due to the study qualification criterion, and 10 were excluded based on data quality concerns.[22] Answers from the remaining 2,510 respondents were used to compute statistics presented in this report, including the tables in appendix C.

The 2015 survey also included an oversample of non-Hispanic black and Hispanic respondents who were randomly selected from KnowledgePanel® respondents in these racial and ethnic groups who did not participate as primary sample respondents in the previous Mobile Survey. Of these additional 1,773 KnowledgePanel® members who received invitations as a part of the non-Hispanic black and Hispanic oversample, 773 people (excluding breakoffs) responded to the e-mail request to participate and completed the survey, yielding a final stage completion rate of 43.6 percent for the oversample. The recruitment rate for the non-Hispanic black and Hispanic oversample, reported by GfK, was 11.6 percent and the profile rate was 64.8 percent, for a cumulative response rate of 3.3 percent. From the 773 oversample respondents who completed the survey, 2 were excluded due to the study qualification criterion, and 2 were excluded based on data quality concerns, yielding 769 responses for analysis. For comparability with the sample design from prior years of

---

[21] For further details on the KnowledgePanel® sampling methodology and comparisons between KnowledgePanel® and telephone surveys see www.knowledgenetworks.com/accuracy/spring2010/disogra-spring10.html.

[22] Respondents who refused to answer whether they own or have regular access to a mobile phone (Q19) were not qualified for the study. Respondents who completed the survey in less than one-fourth of the median time for their respective survey paths or who refused to answer more than one-half of the substantive survey questions were excluded due to data quality concerns.

the Mobile Survey, answers from these respondents are not included in the statistics in this report.

After pretesting, the data collection for the survey began on November 4, 2015. For the re-interviewed sample, the survey was closed to responses on November 9, 2015. For the fresh sample and oversample respondents, the survey concluded on November 23, 2015. To enhance the completion rate, GfK sent e-mail reminders to non-responders from all samples on day three of the field period. Two additional e-mail reminders were sent to the non-responders from the oversample on days 8 and 12 of the field period. Three additional e-mail reminders were sent to the non-responders from the fresh general population sample on days 8, 12, and 16 of the field period. GfK maintains an ongoing modest incentive program to encourage KnowledgePanel® members to participate. Incentives take the form of raffles and lotteries with cash and other prizes.

Significant resources and infrastructure are devoted to the recruitment process for the KnowledgePanel® so that the resulting panel can properly represent the adult population of the United States. Consequently, the raw distribution of KnowledgePanel® mirrors that of U.S. adults fairly closely, barring occasional disparities that may emerge for certain subgroups due to differential attrition rates among recruited panel members.

The selection methodology for general population samples from the KnowledgePanel® ensures that the resulting samples behave as equal probability of selection method (EPSEM) samples. This methodology starts by weighting the entire KnowledgePanel® to the benchmarks secured from the latest March supplement of the Current Population Survey (CPS) along several dimensions. This way, the weighted distribution of the KnowledgePanel® matches that of U.S. adults. Typically, the geo-demographic dimensions used for weighting the entire KnowledgePanel® include gender, age, race/ethnicity, education, Census region, household income, home ownership status, metropolitan area status, and Internet access.

Using the above weights as the measure of size (MOS) for each panel member, in the next step a probability proportional to size (PPS) procedure is used to select study specific samples. For studies that include any oversampling of particular subgroups, the departure from an EPSEM design caused by the oversample is corrected by adjusting the corresponding design weights accordingly with the CPS benchmarks serving as reference points.

Once the sample has been selected and fielded, and all the study data are collected and made final, a post-stratification process is used to adjust for any survey non-response as well as any non-coverage or under- and over-sampling resulting from the study-specific sample design. The following variables were used for the adjustment of weights for this study: gender, age, race/ethnicity, Census region, metropolitan area status, education, and access to the Internet. Demographic and geographic distributions for the general population of adults ages 18 and over from the March 2015 CPS, and the July 2013 CPS for Internet access, were used as benchmarks in this adjustment.

Although weights allow the sample population to match the U.S. population based on observable characteristics, similar to all survey methods, it remains possible that non-coverage or non-response results in differences between the sample population and the U.S. population that are not corrected using weights.

There are several reasons that a probability-based Internet panel was selected as the method for this survey rather than an alternative survey method. The first reason is that these types of Internet surveys have been found to be representative of the population.[23] The second reason is that the ABS Internet panel allows the same respondents to be re-interviewed in subsequent surveys with relative ease, as they remain in the panel for several years. The third reason is that Internet panel surveys have numerous existing data points on respondents from previously administered surveys, including detailed demographic and economic information. This allows for the inclusion of additional information on respondents without increasing respondent burden. Lastly, collecting data through an ABS Internet panel survey is cost effective, and can be done relatively quickly.

There are possible questions about the extent to which results from an online survey of technology use can be interpreted as being representative of the technology use of the U.S. population. As with any

---

[23] David S. Yeager, Jon A. Krosnick, LinChiat Chang, Harold S. Javitz, Matthew S. Levendusky, Alberto Simpser, and Rui Wang, "Comparing the Accuracy of RDD Telephone Surveys and Internet Surveys Conducted with Probability and Non-Probability Samples," *Public Opinion Quarterly* 75, no. 4 (2011):709–47.

survey method, Internet panels can be subject to biases resulting from undercoverage or nonresponse and, in this case, potential underrepresentation of adults who are physically or cognitively impaired or who may prefer not to use some forms of technology.[24] Not everyone in the United States has access to the Internet, and there are demographic (income, education, age) and geographic (urban and rural) differences between those who do have access and those who do not. These concerns about survey error for Internet surveys are partially corrected by GfK providing Internet access to respondents who do not have it in order to include the portion of the population that does not have Internet access in KnowledgePanel®. They are further corrected by the use of post-stratification weights to ensure that the Internet usage and key demographics of the weighted sample population matches the entire U.S. population.

While these steps have been taken to make the survey results generalizable to the adult U.S. population, some caveats apply to interpretation of the results, particularly for subpopulations. This survey was conducted in English, and thus may not reflect the attitudes and behaviors of those in the U.S. population whose dominant language is not English. In addition, participation in this type of survey may require a certain level of skill and interest in responding online, which could limit coverage of some groups, particularly among those in the population who are less likely to use computers or the Internet. As a result, to the extent that these differences cannot be incorporated into the sample weights, technology usage among survey respondents may differ along key dimensions from that of the overall U.S. population.

---

[24] For a discussion of differences in measures from a web-only survey and a web-plus-mail survey design, including a comparison of technology and Internet measures, see Pew Research Center, September 2015, "Coverage Error in Internet Surveys," available at www.pewresearch.org/files/2015/09/2015-09-22_coverage-error-in-internet-surveys.pdf.

Appendix B: Survey of Consumers' Use of Mobile Financial Services 2015—Questionnaire

Below is a reproduction of the survey instrument in its entirety. The bracketed text are programming instructions that (1) indicate whether or not a question is single choice [S] or multiple choice [M] and (2) represent any skip pattern used to reach that question and which questions should be grouped together on a page. The respondents only saw the questions and response options; they did not see the program code.

I. INTRODUCTION

[DISPLAY]

OMB Control Number: 7100-0359

Expiration Date: 04/30/2017

For more information, click here.

The Federal Reserve Board is interested in learning more about how people manage their finances, shop, and make payments. We are also interested in how people interact with financial institutions, and how mobile phones and other technology facilitate these interactions. The information collected in this survey will be used for research, analysis, and policymaking. A dataset containing anonymized responses may also be released publicly on the Federal Reserve Board's website. We appreciate your participation in this survey.

To begin, we are going to ask a few questions about the types of financial products and services that you use.

SCRIPTER: IF "FOR MORE INFORMATION..." CLICKED, DISPLAY THIS TEXT IN A NEW TAB OR WINDOW

The Federal Reserve may not conduct or sponsor, and an organization is not required to respond to, a collection of information unless it displays a currently valid OMB control number. Public reporting burden for this information collection is estimated to average 0.18 hours, including the time to gather data in the required form and to review instructions and complete the information collection. Send comments regarding this burden estimate or any other aspect of this collection of information, including suggestions for reducing this burden to: Secretary, Board of Governors of the Federal Reserve System, 20th and C Streets, NW, Washington, DC 20551, and to the Office of Management and Budget, Paperwork Reduction Project (7100-0359), Washington, DC 20503.

II. MAIN QUESTIONNAIRE

SCRIPTER: USE DEFAULT INSTRUCTION TEXT FOR EACH QUESTION TYPE UNLESS OTHERWISE SPECIFIED.

SCRIPTER: DO NOT PROMPT ON ALL QUESTIONS.

Standard response labels include:

S = Single Select (only one answer possible)

M = Multi Select (multiple answers are possible)

Grid = Grid (one answer per row assumed by default, specify if other response type needed)

Q = Quantity (numeric response)

O = Open End (free form text response; indicate size of text response box)

OL = Open List (text response boxes for unaided recall; 10 boxes set-up as standard)

A. Banking Section

Base: All respondents

Q1 [S]

Do you **[IF PPMARIT=1, INSERT:**"and/or your spouse" **/ IF PPMARIT=6, INSERT:**"and/or your partner"**]** currently have a checking, savings or money market account?

1. Yes
2. No

Base: Q1=2

Q2 [S]

Have you **[IF PPMARIT=1, INSERT:**"and/or your spouse"**/ IF PPMARIT=6, INSERT:**"and/or your partner"**]** ever had a checking, savings or money market account?

1. Yes
2. No

Base: All respondents

Q3 [S]

Have you used a **general-purpose reloadable prepaid card** in the past 12 months? General-purpose reloadable prepaid cards typically have a Visa, MasterCard, American Express, or Discover logo and can be used like debit cards to purchase goods in stores and online, pay bills, and withdraw cash from an ATM. Money must be loaded onto the card before it is used, and the card can be reloaded with money as well. (Please do NOT include nonreloadable cards, such as gift and rebate cards.)

1. Yes
2. No

Base: All respondents

Q4 [GRID]

SCRIPTER: SHOW THIS TEXT INSTEAD OF DEFAULT INSTRUCTIONS: Please answer yes or no to each option

In the past 12 months, have you:

Statement in row:

1. used a money order
2. used a check-cashing service
3. used a tax refund anticipation loan
4. used a pawn shop loan, a payday loan, an auto title loan, or a paycheck advance/deposit advance
5. sent money to a relative or friend (not a business) living outside of the U.S. using a service other than a bank (e.g. WesternUnion, USPS SureMoney, etc.)

Answers in column:

1. Yes
2. No

Base: IF Q1 = 1

[DISPLAY; SHOW ON THE SAME SCREEN AS Q5]

In this section we would like to ask you about how you interact with your bank or credit union.

Base: IF Q1 = 1

SCRIPTER: ALLOW RESPONDENTS TO CHOOSE UP TO 3 ANSWER OPTIONS. REPLACE DEFAULT INSTRUCTIONS WITH: Select up to 3 answers

Q5 [M – allow 3 selections maximum]

SCRIPTER: RANGE: 1–3; Unique Values; SHOW ON SAME SCREEN AS DISPLAY, USE SAME FORMAT AS Q16 in SNO19247, NOTE RANGE CHANGE

What do you consider to be the most important ways you interact with your bank or credit union?

1. ATM/Cash machine
2. A teller in person at a branch
3. Over the internet using a computer/tablet
4. Mobile phone app, mobile web browser or SMS/text message
5. Phone – Talking or using touchtone service
6. Mail
7. Family member, friend, or neighbor does the banking for me
8. Other (Please specify):[TXT]_____

Base: IF Q1 = 1

Q6 [S]

Have you visited a bank branch and spoken with **a teller or a bank employee** in the past 12 months? Please do not include visits where your only activity was using an ATM/Cash machine located at a branch.

1. Yes
2. No

Base: Q6 = 1

Q7 [Q; RANGE: 0-99]

In the past **month**, about how many times have you visited a branch and spoken with a teller or a bank employee? If none enter "0".

_____times in the past month

Base: Q1 = 1

Q8 [Q; RANGE: 0-999]

About how long does it take you to travel to the branch you typically visit (one way)?

_____ minutes

☐ Check this box if you don't visit a branch [S]

Base: Respondents who chose checkbox for Q8

Q8a [S]

Which of the following best describes the location of your bank or credit union branch where you can speak with a teller or bank employee, if needed?

1. I have a branch close to my home, work, school, or other place I go frequently.
2. I must go out of my way or travel for a while to visit a branch.
3. I am not able to visit a branch because my bank does not have a branch in my area.

Base: Q6 = 1

Q9 [GRID]

SCRIPTER: SHOW THIS TEXT INSTEAD OF DEFAULT INSTRUCTIONS: Please answer yes or no to each option

In the past 12 months when you visited a branch and spoke with a teller or customer service representative, did you do each of the following in any of those visits? (Please do not include ATM/Cash machine transactions.)

Statement in row:

1. Deposit a check or cash
2. Withdraw cash/cash a check
3. Get a cashier's check, certified check, or money order
4. Send/wire money to someone
5. Transfer money between accounts
6. Apply for a loan
7. Open or close an account
8. Resolve a problem or question or get general information about products or services
9. Get specific information about your account (e.g., balance, recent activity)
10. Other (please specify): **[TXT]**

Answers in column:

1. Yes
2. No

Base: Q1 = 1

Q10 [S]

Have you used an **ATM** for any banking transactions in the past 12 months?

1. Yes
2. No

Base: Q10 = 1

Q11 [Q; RANGE: 0-99]

In the past **month**, about how many times have you used an **ATM** for banking transactions? If none enter "0".

_____times in the past month

Base: Q1 = 1

Q12 [Q; RANGE: 0-999]

About how long does it take you to travel to the ATM you typically use (one way)?

____minutes

☐ Check this box if you don't use an ATM.[S]

Base: Respondents who chose checkbox for Q12

Q12a [S]

Which of the following best describes the location of the ATM you can use for banking transactions, if needed?

1. I have an ATM close to my home, work, school, or other place I go frequently.
2. I must go out of my way or travel for a while to access the ATM.
3. I am not able to use an ATM for banking transactions because there is not an ATM in my area.

Base: Q1 = 1

Q13 [S]

Telephone banking is when you access your account by calling a phone number that your bank has provided. You interact with the system using either voice commands, your phone's numeric keypad, or speaking with a live customer service representative. It does not include accessing your bank using the internet or apps on your mobile phone.

Have you used telephone banking in the past 12 months, either with a land-line phone or your mobile phone?

1. Yes
2. No

Base: Q13 = 1

Q14 [Q; RANGE: 0-99]

In the past **month**, about how many times have you used **telephone banking** to access your account? If none enter "0".

_____times in the past month

Base: All respondents

[DISPLAY; SHOW ON THE SAME SCREEN AS Q15]

In this section, we'll ask a few questions about your use of the internet. Right now we are just interested in your use of the internet **on a computer** (desktop, laptop) or **tablet**. Later on we will ask about use of the internet on mobile phones.

Base: All respondents

Q15 [GRID]

SCRIPTER: SHOW THIS TEXT INSTEAD OF DEFAULT INSTRUCTIONS: Please answer yes or no to each option

Do you currently have **regular access to the internet at your home** that is not provided by GfK, formerly Knowledge Networks?

Statement in row:

1. Using a computer (desktop, laptop)?
2. Using a tablet (e.g., iPad)?

Answers in column:

1. Yes
2. No

Base: All respondents

Q16 [GRID]

SCRIPTER: SHOW THIS TEXT INSTEAD OF DEFAULT INSTRUCTIONS: Please answer yes or no to each option

Do you currently have **regular access to the internet outside your home** (e.g., at school, work, public library, etc.)?

Statement in row:

1. Using a computer (desktop, laptop)?
2. Using a tablet (e.g., iPad)?

Answers in column:

1. Yes
2. No

Base: Q1=1

Q17 [S]

Online banking involves checking your account balance and recent transactions, transferring money, paying bills, or conducting other related transactions with your bank or credit union using the internet.

Have you used online banking on a desktop, laptop, or tablet (e.g., iPad) computer in the past 12 months?

1. Yes
2. No

Base: Q17=1

Q18 [Q; RANGE: 0-99]

In the past **month**, about how many times have you used online banking on a desktop, laptop, or tablet (e.g., iPad) computer? If none enter "0".

_____times in the past month

B. Mobile Phone Usage

Base: All respondents

[DISPLAY; SHOW ON SAME SCREEN AS Q19]

In this section we would like to ask you about your use of mobile phones (cell phones).

Base: All respondents

Q19 [S][PROMPT, TERMINATE IF SKIPPED]

Do you own or have regular access to a mobile phone (cell phone)?

1. Yes ♦ [MOBILE = "YES"]
2. No ♦ [MOBILE = "NO"]

SCRIPTER: TERMINATE IF REFUSED Q19

CREATE DOV: MOBILE

DOV_MOBILE =1 IF Q19=1

DOV_MOBILE =2 IF Q19=2

Base: DOV_MOBILE=1

Q20 [S]

A **smartphone** is a mobile phone with features that may enable it to access the web, send e-mails, download apps, and interact with computers. Smartphones include the iPhone, Blackberry, as well as Android and Windows Mobile powered devices.

Is your mobile phone a smartphone?

1. Yes
2. No

Base: Q20=1

Q21 [S]

Which type of smartphone do you have?

1. Android
2. Blackberry
3. iPhone
4. Windows Mobile
5. Other
6. Don't know

Base: DOV_MOBILE=1

Q22 [S]

How confident are you in your ability to understand and navigate the technology and features of your mobile phone?

1. Very confident
2. Somewhat confident
3. Not confident

Base: Q20=1

Q23 [S]

Do you password protect your smart phone? Please count using a PIN, drawing a pattern, fingerprint or facial recognition, and other methods of securing your phone as password protection.

1. Yes
2. No

Base: Q20=1

Q24 [GRID]

SCRIPTER: SHOW THIS TEXT INSTEAD OF DEFAULT INSTRUCTIONS: Please answer yes or no to each option

In the past 12 months, have you taken any of the following actions with your smartphone?

PROGRAMMING NOTE: CODE "Yes" AS 1, "No" AS 0, AND REFUSED AS -1.

Statement in row:

1. Install updates to your mobile operating system or your apps
2. Change password on your phone or apps
3. Use anti-malware software or other means to protect your smartphone
4. Download or install apps from sources **outside** the primary app store for your phone (e.g., from sources **other than** Apple iTunes, Google Play, or Windows Phone stores)
5. Customize privacy settings (e.g., restricting which apps can track your location)
6. Password protect apps that store sensitive data (e.g., mobile wallet)
7. Send or access sensitive data over public WiFi networks
8. Use an app or other service that allows you to locate, remotely access, erase, or disable your smartphone in case of loss or theft (e.g., Apple "Find my iPhone" or BullGuard)

Answer in columns:

1. Yes
2. No

C. Mobile Banking Users

Base: DOV_MOBILE=1 AND Q1=1

[DISPLAY; SHOW ON THE SAME SCREEN AS Q25 and Q26]

Mobile banking uses a mobile phone to access your bank or credit union account. This can be done either by accessing your bank or credit union's web page through the web browser on your mobile phone, via text messaging, or by using an app downloaded to your mobile phone.

Base: DOV_MOBILE=1 AND Q1=1

Q25 [S; SHOWN ON SAME SCREEN AS Q26]

Does your bank or credit union offer mobile banking?

1. Yes
2. No
3. Don't know

Base: DOV_MOBILE=1 AND Q1=1

Q26 [S; SHOWN ON SAME SCREEN AS Q25]

Have you used **mobile banking** in the past 12 months?

1. Yes ♦ [MOBILEBANK = "YES"]
2. No ♦ [MOBILEBANK = "NO"]

CREATE DOV: MOBILEBANK

1. "YES"
2. "NO"

Base: DOV_MOBILEBANK=2

Q27 [S]

Do you plan to use mobile banking in the next 12 months?

1. Definitely will use
2. Probably will use
3. Probably will not use
4. Definitely will not use

Base: DOV_MOBILE=1 AND Q1=1

Q28 [GRID]

SCRIPTER: SHOW THIS TEXT INSTEAD OF DEFAULT INSTRUCTIONS: Please answer yes or no to each option

Using your **mobile phone**, have you done each of the following in the past 12 months?

PROGRAMMING NOTE: CODE "Yes" AS 1, "No" AS 0, AND REFUSED AS -1.

Statement in rows:

1. Checked an account balance or checked recent transactions
2. Made a bill payment using your bank's online banking website or banking app
3. Received an alert (e.g., a text message, push notification or email) from your bank
4. Transferred money between your bank accounts
5. Sent money to relatives or friends **within the U.S.** using your bank's app or mobile website
6. Sent money to relatives or friends **outside the U.S.** using your bank's app or mobile website
7. Deposited a check to your account electronically using your mobile phone camera
8. Located the closest in-network ATM or branch for your bank

Answers in columns:

1. Yes
2. No

Base: DOV_MOBILE=1 AND Q1=1

Q29 [S]

Do you have your bank's mobile banking app on your mobile phone?

1. Yes
2. No

Base: DOV_MOBILEBANK=1

Q30 [Q; RANGE: 0-999]

In the past **month**, about how many times have you personally used mobile banking? If none enter "0".

_____ times in the past month

Base: DOV_MOBILEBANK=1

SCRIPTER: SHOW ON THE SAME SCREEN AS Q30

Q31 [S]

When did you start using mobile banking?

1. In the last 6 months
2. 6 to 12 months ago
3. 1 to 2 years ago
4. More than 2 years ago
5. I don't remember

Base: DOV_MOBILEBANK=1

Q32 [S]

What was the **main** reason why you started using mobile banking when you did?

1. I got a smartphone
2. My bank started offering the service
3. There is no bank branch or ATM near my home or work
4. I became comfortable with the security of mobile banking
5. I liked the convenience of mobile banking
6. To receive fraud alerts or check my account for fraudulent transactions
7. Other (Please specify):**[TXT]**_____

D. Mobile Payments Users

Base: DOV_MOBILE=1

[DISPLAY; SHOW ON THE SAME SCREEN AS Q33]

Mobile payments are purchases, bill payments, charitable donations, payments to another person, or any other payments made using a mobile phone. This includes using your phone to pay for something in a store as well as payments made through an app, a mobile web browser or a text message.

Base: DOV_MOBILE=1

Q33 [S] [MOBILE = "YES"]

Have you made a **mobile payment** in the past 12 months?

1. Yes ♦ [MOBILEPAY = "YES"]
2. No ♦ [MOBILEPAY = "NO"]

CREATE DOV: MOBILEPAY

1. "YES"
2. "NO"

Base: DOV_MOBILE=1

Q34 [GRID]

SCRIPTER: SHOW THIS TEXT INSTEAD OF DEFAULT INSTRUCTIONS: Please answer yes or no to each option

Using your **mobile phone**, have you done each of the following in the past 12 months? Please include payments you made through your bank as well as through other companies that are not your bank.

PROGRAMMING NOTE: CODE "Yes" AS 1, "No" AS 0, AND REFUSED AS -1.

Statement in rows:

1. Sent money to relatives or friends **within the U.S.** (e.g., Venmo, PayPal, Google Wallet, your bank's app)
2. Sent money to relatives or friends **outside the U.S.** (e.g., WesternUnion or USPS SureMoney, your bank's app)
3. Paid for something in a store using your mobile phone/app (e.g., Starbucks, Apple Pay) instead of cash or a physical payment card
4. Paid for parking, a taxi, car service (e.g., Uber), or public transit
5. Paid a bill using your mobile phone's web browser or an app
6. Purchased a physical item or digital content remotely by using your mobile phone's web browser or an app
7. Made a donation or other payment using a text message

Answer in columns:

1. Yes
2. No

Base: DOV_MOBILEPAY=1

SCRIPTER: SHOW Q35 AND Q36 ON THE SAME SCREEN

Q35 [Q; RANGE: 0-99]

In the past **month**, about how many times have you used your mobile phone to make any type of mobile payment? If none please enter "0".

_____times in the past month

Base: Q34C=1

Q36 [Q; RANGE: 0-99]

In the past **month**, about how many times have you used your mobile phone to pay for a product or service at a store? If none please enter "0".

_____times in the past month

Base: Q34C=2

Q34a [S]

You indicated that you have not made a mobile payment in a store in the past 12 months. Do you plan to use your mobile phone to make a payment in a store in the next 12 months?

1. Definitely will use
2. Probably will use
3. Probably will not use
4. Definitely will not use

Base: DOV_MOBILEPAY=1

Q37 [M]

When making mobile payments, which of the following payment methods do you use?

1. Credit card
2. Debit card
3. Prepaid debit card
4. Bank account
5. Charge to your phone bill
6. Account at a non-financial institution (e.g., PayPal)
7. Other (Please specify):[TXT]_____

Base: DOV_MOBILEPAY=1

SCRIPTER: SHOW ON THE SAME SCREEN AS Q39

Q38 [S]

When did you start using mobile payments?

1. In the last 6 months
2. 6 to 12 months ago
3. 1 to 2 years ago
4. More than 2 years ago
5. I don't remember

Base: DOV_MOBILEPAY=1

SCRIPTER: SHOW ON THE SAME SCREEN AS Q38

Q39 [S]

What was the **main** reason why you started using mobile payments when you did?

1. I got a smartphone
2. The ability to make mobile payments became available
3. I became comfortable with the security of mobile payments
4. I liked the convenience of mobile payments
5. A store I visit started offering the service
6. To take advantage of loyalty or rewards points and discounts
7. Other (Please specify):**[TXT]**_____

E. Non-Mobile Banking Users

Base: DOV_MOBILEBANK=2 AND Q25=1

[DISPLAY; SHOW ON SAME PAGE AS Q40]

We would like to ask you about some of your reasons for not using mobile banking.

Base: DOV_MOBILEBANK=2 AND Q25=1

Q40 [GRID]

SCRIPTER: SHOW THIS TEXT INSTEAD OF DEFAULT INSTRUCTIONS: Please answer yes or no to each option

Please tell us if each of the reasons below are why you do not use mobile banking.

PROGRAMMING NOTE: CODE "Yes" AS 1, "No" AS 0, AND REFUSED AS -1.

Statements in rows:

1. I'm concerned about the security of mobile banking
2. My banking needs are being met without mobile banking
3. I don't see any reason to use mobile banking
4. The mobile phone screen is too small
5. I don't have a smartphone
6. My bank charges a fee for using mobile banking
7. I don't do the banking in my household
8. I don't trust the technology
9. It's too difficult to use mobile banking

Answers in columns:

1. Yes
2. No

Base: DOV_MOBILEBANK=2 AND Q25=1

Q41 [M]

Assuming that the concerns that you have about using mobile banking were addressed, would you be interested in doing any of the following activities with your mobile phone?

1. Download your bank's mobile banking app
2. Check an account balance or recent transactions
3. Make bill payments using your bank's website or app
4. Receive alerts (e.g., text message, push notification or email) from your bank
5. Deposit a check electronically using a mobile phone camera
6. Transfer money between your bank accounts
7. Send money to relatives or friends **within the U.S.**
8. Send money to relatives or friends **outside the U.S.**
9. Locate the closest in-network ATM or branch
10. None, I don't want to use mobile banking **[Exclusive]**

Base: Q25=2 OR Q25=3

Q42 [M]

You mentioned that your bank does not offer mobile banking or you are not sure if you bank offers it. If your bank or credit union were to offer mobile banking, would you be interested in doing any of the following activities with your mobile phone?

1. Download your bank's mobile banking app
2. Check an account balance or recent transactions
3. Make bill payments using your bank's website or app
4. Receive alerts (e.g., text message, push notification or email) from your bank
5. Deposit a check electronically using a mobile phone camera
6. Transfer money between your accounts
7. Send money to relatives or friends **within the U.S.**
8. Send money to relatives or friends **outside the U.S.**
9. Locate the closest in-network ATM or branch
10. None, I don't want to use mobile banking **[Exclusive]**

F. Non-Mobile Payments Users

Base: DOV_MOBILEPAY=2

[DISPLAY; shown on the same page as Q43]

We would like to ask you about some of your reasons for not using mobile payments.

Base: DOV_MOBILEPAY=2 AND DOV_MOBILE=1

Q43 [GRID]

SCRIPTER: SHOW THIS TEXT INSTEAD OF DEFAULT INSTRUCTIONS: Please answer yes or no to each option

Please tell us if any of the reasons below are why you do not use mobile payments.

PROGRAMMING NOTE: CODE "Yes" AS 1, "No" AS 0, AND REFUSED AS -1.

Statements in rows:

1. I'm concerned about the security of mobile payments
2. It's easier to pay with cash or a credit/debit card
3. I don't see any benefit from using mobile payments
4. The places I shop don't accept mobile payments
5. I don't have the necessary feature on my phone
6. I don't trust the technology
7. It's difficult or time consuming to set up or use mobile payments
8. I don't need to make any payments or someone else pays the bills
9. I don't really understand all the different mobile payment options

Answers in columns:

1. Yes
2. No

Base: DOV_MOBILEPAY=2

Q44 [M]

Assuming that the reason(s) why you do not currently use mobile payments was addressed, would you be interested in doing any of the following activities with your mobile phone?

1. Sending money to relatives or friends **within the U.S.**
2. Sending money to relatives or friends **outside the U.S.**
3. Paying for something in a store using your mobile phone/app instead of cash or a physical payment card
4. Paying for parking, a taxi, car service or public transit
5. Paying a bill using your mobile phone's web browser or an app
6. Purchasing a physical item or digital content remotely by using your mobile phone's web browser or an app
7. Making a donation or other payment using a text message
8. None, I don't want to use mobile payments [S]

G. Mobile Financial Services Security Questions

Base: DOV_MOBILE=1

[DISPLAY; SHOW ON THE SAME SCREEN WITH Q45 AND Q46]

Please rate your perception of the level of security for each of the following mobile financial services from Very Safe to Very Unsafe.

Base: DOV_MOBILE=1

SCRIPTER: SHOW ON THE SAME SCREEN AS Q46

Q45 [S]

How safe do you believe people's personal information is when they use mobile banking?

1. Very safe
2. Somewhat safe
3. Somewhat unsafe
4. Very unsafe
5. Don't know

Base: DOV_MOBILE=1

SCRIPTER: SHOW ON THE SAME SCREEN AS Q45

Q46 [S]

How safe do you believe people's personal information is when they use a mobile phone to pay for a purchase at a store?

1. Very safe
2. Somewhat safe
3. Somewhat unsafe
4. Very unsafe
5. Don't know

Base: DOV_MOBILE=1

Q47 [S]

Which one of the following security aspects would cause you the most concern about using your mobile phone for financial transactions such as mobile banking or paying for a purchase in a store?

1. My phone getting hacked or someone intercepting my data
2. Someone using my phone without permission to access my account
3. Losing my phone or having my phone stolen
4. Malware or viruses being installed on my phone
5. Companies misusing my personal information
6. Companies (merchants, banks, third parties) not providing sufficient security to protect my mobile transactions
7. All of the above
8. Other (Please specify): **[TXT][ADD SPACE]**
9. No concerns/I think it is safe

Base: DOV_MOBILE=1

Q48 [GRID]

Do you already use, would like to use, or are unlikely to use your mobile phone for each of the following purposes?

Statements in rows:

1. Track your finances, purchases or expenses
2. Organize, track and store gift cards, memberships, loyalty and reward points
3. Compare prices when shopping
4. Receive and manage discount offers and coupons
5. Receive offers and promotions based on your location

Answers in columns:

1. I already do
2. I would like to
3. I am unlikely to

Base: Q20=1

[DISPLAY; SHOW ON THE SAME SCREEN AS Q49 and Q50]

For the following two questions please rate how much you agree or disagree with the statement on a scale from strongly agree to strongly disagree.

Base: Q20=1

SCRIPTER: SHOW ON THE SAME SCREEN AS Q50

Q49 [S]

I am willing to allow my mobile phone to provide my location to companies I shop with regularly so that they can offer me discounts, promotions, or services based on where I am.

1. Strongly agree
2. Agree
3. Disagree
4. Strongly disagree

Base: Q20=1

SCRIPTER: SHOW ON THE SAME SCREEN AS Q49

Q50 [S]

I am willing to answer security questions or provide additional information to my bank or credit union when I log into mobile banking so that my bank can enhance the security of my mobile transaction.

1. Strongly agree
2. Agree
3. Disagree
4. Strongly disagree

H. Shopping Behavior Questions

Base: DOV_MOBILE=1 AND Q20=1

SCRIPTER: SHOW ON SAME SCREEN AS Q51

[DISPLAY]

In this section, we would like to ask you about your shopping habits.

Base: DOV_MOBILE=1 AND Q20=1

SCRIPTER: SHOW ON SAME SCREEN AS Q52

Q51 [S]

Have you ever used your mobile phone to comparison shop over the internet while at a retail store?

1. Yes
2. No

Base: DOV_MOBILE=1 AND Q20=1

SCRIPTER: SHOW ON SAME SCREEN AS Q51

Q52 [S]

Have you ever used a barcode scanning app on your mobile phone while shopping at a retail store to find the best price for an item?

1. Yes
2. No

Base: Q51=1 OR Q52=1

Q53 [S]

Has using your mobile phone to compare prices while you were shopping at a retail store ever changed where you made your purchase?

1. Yes
2. No

Base: DOV_MOBILE=1 AND Q20=1

SCRIPTER: SHOWN ON THE SAME SCREEN AS Q55

Q54 [S]

Have you ever scanned a QR code (similar to a barcode) in a retail store, newspaper, magazine, or billboard advertisement to obtain information about a product on your mobile phone?

1. Yes
2. No

Base: DOV_MOBILE=1 AND Q20=1

SCRIPTER: SHOWN ON THE SAME SCREEN AS Q54

Q55 [S]

Have you ever used your mobile phone to browse product reviews or get product information while shopping at a retail store? This could be done by, for example, googling the product on your mobile browser or scanning a QR code.

1. Yes
2. No

Base: Q55=1

Q56 [S]

Has reading product reviews on your mobile phone while shopping at a retail store ever changed which item you ended up purchasing?

1. Yes
2. No

Base: DOV_MOBILEBANK=1 AND Q20=1

Q57 [S]

In the past 12 months, have you used your mobile phone to check your account balance or available credit before making a large purchase?

1. Yes
2. No

Base: Q57=1

Q58 [S]

Thinking of the most recent time that you checked your account balance or available credit before making a large purchase, did you decide not to buy that particular item because of the amount of money left in your account or the amount of your available credit?

1. Yes
2. No

I. Financial Management (Saving, Budgeting) Questions

Base: Q28C=1

Q59 [M]

You previously mentioned that you receive text message, push notification or email alerts from your financial institution. Do you receive each of the following kinds of alerts?

1. Low balance
2. Payment due
3. Saving reminders
4. Fraud
5. Credit card balance
6. Deposit or withdrawal
7. Statement available notification
8. Other (Please specify):[TXT]_____

Base: Q59=1

Q60 [M]

Thinking of the most recent low-balance alert you received, which of the following actions did you take after receiving the alert?

1. Transferred money into the account with the low balance from another account
2. Deposited money into the account with the low balance
3. Reduced my spending
4. None of the above **[S]**

III. STANDARD SCREENED OUT TEXT FOR PANEL SAMPLE

<INSERT STANDARD CLOSE>

END OF QUESTIONNAIRE

Appendix C: Consumer Responses to Survey Questionnaire

These questions in these tables may not present the full question as seen by respondents, as some were shortened for presentation purposes. For the full context of each question, including definitions provided to survey respondents and instructions regarding which respondents were asked each question, please see the questionnaire in appendix B.

Table C.1. Do you [or you partner/spouse] currently have a checking, savings, or money market account?

Q1 response	Percent, except as noted
Refused	0.3
Yes	90.6
No	9.1
Number of respondents	2,510

Table C.2. Have you [or you partner/spouse] ever had a checking, savings, or money market account?

Q2 response	Percent, except as noted
Yes	49.8
No	50.2
Number of respondents	128

Table C.3. Have you used a general-purpose reloadable prepaid card in the past 12 months?

Q3 response	Percent, except as noted
Refused	0.6
Yes	16.2
No	83.2
Number of respondents	2,510

Table C.4. In the past 12 months, have you:

Q4 response	Percent, except as noted
Refused	0.1
Used a money order	20.9
Used a check-cashing service	8.9
Used a tax refund anticipation loan	2.3
Used a pawn shop loan, a payday loan, an auto title loan, or a paycheck advance/deposit advance	6.1
Sent money to a relative or friend (not a business) living outside of the U.S. using a service other than a bank	6.2
Number of respondents	2,510

Table C.5. What do you consider to be the most important ways you interact with your bank or credit union?

Q5 response	Percent, except as noted
Refused	0.2
ATM/Cash machine	56.8
A teller in person at a branch	67.5
Over the Internet using a computer/tablet	51.4
Mobile phone app, mobile web browser or SMS/text message	22.4
Phone - Talking or using touchtone service	18.8
Mail	6.4
Family member, friend, or neighbor does the banking for me	2.4
Other	0.2*
Number of respondents	2,373

* Fewer than 10 responses were received for this option.

Table C.6. Have you visited a bank branch and spoken with a teller or a bank employee in the past 12 months?

Q6 response	Percent, except as noted
Refused	0.2
Yes	84.1
No	15.8
Number of respondents	2,373

Table C.7. In the past month, about how many times have you visited a branch and spoken with a teller or a bank employee?

Q7 response	Percent, except as noted
Refused	0.5
Share of respondents with zero uses	19.7
Mean number of uses (at least one use)	2.9
Median number of uses (at least one use)	2.0
Number of respondents	2,042

Table C.8. About how long does it take you to travel to the branch you typically visit (one way)?

Q8 response	Percent, except as noted
Refused	0.4
Mean number of minutes	10.6
Median number of minutes	10.0
Don't visit a branch	6.2
Number of respondents	2,373

Table C.9. Which of the following best describes the location of your bank or credit union branch where you can speak with a teller or bank employee, if needed?

Q8a response	Percent, except as noted
Refused	1.2
I have a branch close to my home, work, school, or other place I go frequently.	34.2
I must go out of my way or travel for a while to visit a branch.	19.2
I am not able to visit a branch because my bank does not have a branch in my area.	45.4
Number of respondents	116

Table C.10. In the past 12 months when you visited a branch and spoke with a teller or customer service representative, did you do each of the following in any of those visits?

Q9 response	Percent, except as noted
Refused/no to all	1.1
Deposit a check or cash	77.7
Withdraw cash/cash a check	65.9
Get a cashier's check, certified check, or money order	13.1
Send/wire money to someone	2.9
Transfer money between accounts	21.1
Apply for a loan	6.4
Open or close an account	13.2
Resolve a problem or question or get general information about products or services	24.6
Get specific information about your account (e.g., balance, recent activity)	25.1
Other	4.7
Number of respondents	2,042

Note: "Other" write-in responses that were repetitions of the main nine response options were reclassified into the correct categories, and the "Other" category was set to a "No" response.

Table C.11. Have you used an ATM for any banking transactions in the past 12 months?

Q10 response	Percent, except as noted
Refused	0.1
Yes	75.4
No	24.5
Number of respondents	2,373

Table C.12. In the past month, about how many times have you used an ATM for banking transactions?

Q11 response	Percent, except as noted
Refused	0.5
Share of respondents with zero uses	13.6
Mean number of uses (at least one use)	4.6
Median number of uses (at least one use)	3.0
Number of respondents	1,769

Table C.13. About how long does it take you to travel to the ATM you typically use (one way)?

Q12 response	Percent, except as noted
Refused	0.6
Mean number of minutes	8.4
Median number of minutes	5.0
Don't use an ATM	16.5
Number of respondents	2,373

Table C.14. Which of the following best describes the location of the ATM you can use for banking transactions, if needed?

Q12a response	Percent, except as noted
Refused	7.6
I have an ATM close to my home, work, school, or other place I go frequently.	68.8
I must go out of my way or travel for a while to access the ATM.	12.0
I am not able to use an ATM for banking transactions because there is not an ATM in my area.	11.6
Number of respondents	421

Table C.15. Have you used telephone banking in the past 12 months, either with a land-line phone or your mobile phone?

Q13 response	Percent, except as noted
Refused	0.2
Yes	29.7
No	70.2
Number of respondents	2,373

Table C.16. In the past month, about how many times have you used telephone banking to access your account?

Q14 response	Percent, except as noted
Refused	0.1
Share of respondents with zero uses	30.1
Mean number of uses (at least one use)	4.4
Median number of uses (at least one use)	2.0
Number of respondents	651

Table C.17. Do you currently have regular access to the Internet at your home that is not provided by GfK, formerly Knowledge Networks?

Q15 response	Percent, except as noted
Refused	0.2
Using a computer (desktop, laptop)	78.3
Using a tablet (e.g., iPad)	42.3
Neither	17.6
Number of respondents	2,510

Table C.18. Do you currently have regular access to the Internet outside your home (e.g., at school, work, public library, etc.)?

Q16 response	Percent, except as noted
Refused	0.3
Using a computer (desktop, laptop)	57.2
Using a tablet (e.g., iPad)	28.4
Neither	38.3
Number of respondents	2,510

Table C.19. Have you used online banking on a desktop, laptop, or tablet (e.g., iPad) computer in the past 12 months?

Q17 response	Percent, except as noted
Refused	0.6
Yes	71.1
No	28.3
Number of respondents	2,373

Table C.20. In the past month, about how many times have you used online banking on a desktop, laptop, or tablet (e.g., iPad) computer?

Q18 response	Percent, except as noted
Refused	0.1
Share of respondents with zero uses	4.7
Mean number of uses (at least one use)	9.0
Median number of uses (at least one use)	5.0
Number of respondents	1,772

Table C.21. Do you own or have regular access to a mobile phone (cell phone)?

Q19 response	Percent, except as noted
Yes	87.4
No	12.6
Number of respondents	2,510

Table C.22. Is your mobile phone a smartphone?

Q20 response	Percent, except as noted
Refused	0.3
Yes	76.6
No	23.2
Number of respondents	2,244

Table C.23. Which type of smartphone do you have?

Q21 response	Percent, except as noted
Refused	0.0
Android	50.6
BlackBerry	0.8
iPhone	41.7
Windows Mobile	2.3
Other	2.6
Don't know	2.0
Number of respondents	1,680

Table C.24. How confident are you in your ability to understand and navigate the technology and features of your mobile phone?

Q22 response	Percent, except as noted
Refused	0.4
Very confident	51.3
Somewhat confident	37.2
Not confident	11.2
Number of respondents	2,244

Table C.25. Do you password protect your smartphone?

Q23 response	Percent, except as noted
Refused	0.6
Yes	69.9
No	29.5
Number of respondents	1,680

Table C.26. In the past 12 months, have you taken any of the following actions with your smartphone?

Q24 response	Percent, except as noted
Refused/no to all	10.4
Install updates to your mobile operating system or your apps	83.8
Change password on your phone or apps	43.4
Use anti-malware software/apps or other means to protect your smartphone	32.9
Download or install apps from sources outside the primary app store for your phone	21.3
Customize privacy settings (e.g., restricting which apps can track your location)	57.8
Password protect apps that store sensitive data, e.g., mobile wallet	38.9
Send or access sensitive data over public WiFi networks	23.1
Use an app or other service that allows you to locate, remotely access, erase, or disable your smartphone in case of loss or theft (e.g., Apple "Find my iPhone" or BullGuard)	32.9
Number of respondents	1,680

Table C.27. Does your bank or credit union offer mobile banking?

Q25 response	Percent, except as noted
Refused	0.1
Yes	74.7
No	4.6
Don't know	20.6
Number of respondents	2,151

Table C.28. Have you used mobile banking in the past 12 months?

Q26 response	Percent, except as noted
Refused	0.6
Yes	42.7
No	56.7
Number of respondents	2,151

Table C.29. Do you plan to use mobile banking in the next 12 months?

Q27 response	Percent, except as noted
Refused	0.4
Definitely will use	0.7*
Probably will use	11.5
Probably will not use	43.7
Definitely will not use	43.7
Number of respondents	1,343

* Fewer than 10 responses were received for this option.

Table C.30. Using your mobile phone, have you done each of the following in the past 12 months?

Q28 response	Percent, except as noted
Refused/no to all	42.3
Checked an account balance or checked recent transactions	49.6
Made a bill payment using your bank's online banking website or banking app	23.4
Received an alert (e.g., a text message, push notification, or e-mail) from your bank	31.2
Transferred money between your bank accounts	28.0
Sent money to relatives or friends within the U.S. using your bank's app or mobile website	7.4
Sent money to relatives or friends outside the U.S. using your bank's app or mobile website	1.8
Deposited a check to your account electronically using your mobile phone camera	21.7
Located the closest in-network ATM or branch for your bank	19.9
Number of respondents	2,151

Note: This question was asked of those with a mobile phone and a bank account and includes those who did not identify themselves as having used mobile banking in the previous 12 months.

Table C.31. Do you have your bank's mobile banking app on your mobile phone?

Q29 response	Percent, except as noted
Refused	0.7
Yes	39.8
No	59.5
Number of respondents	2,151

Table C.32. In the past month, about how many times have you personally used mobile banking?

Q30 response	Percent, except as noted
Refused	1.8
Share of respondents with zero uses	9.4
Mean number of uses (at least one use)	9.3
Median number of uses (at least one use)	5.0
Number of respondents	801

Table C.33. When did you start using mobile banking?

Q31 response	Percent, except as noted
Refused	6.0
In the last 6 months	9.1
6 to 12 months ago	13.8
1 to 2 years ago	25.5
More than 2 years ago	38.7
I don't remember	7.0
Number of respondents	801

Table C.34. What was the main reason why you started using mobile banking when you did?

Q32 response	Percent, except as noted
Refused	0.5
I got a smartphone	25.8
My bank started offering the service	19.0
There is no bank branch or ATM near my home or work	3.4
I became comfortable with the security of mobile banking	6.7
I liked the convenience of mobile banking	38.8
To receive fraud alerts or check my account for fraudulent transactions	2.9
Other	2.9
Number of respondents	801

Table C.35. Have you made a mobile payment in the past 12 months?

Q33 response	Percent, except as noted
Refused	0.3
Yes	23.7
No	76.0
Number of respondents	2,244

Table C.36. Using your mobile phone, have you done each of the following in the past 12 months?

Q34 response	Percent, except as noted
Refused/no to all	70.1
Sent money to relatives or friends within the U.S. (e.g., Venmo, PayPal, Google Wallet, your bank's app)	8.3
Sent money to relatives or friends outside the U.S. (e.g., Western Union or USPS SureMoney, your bank's app)	2.6
Paid for something in a store using your mobile phone/app (e.g., Starbucks, Apple Pay) instead of cash or a physical payment card	9.9
Paid for parking, a taxi, car service (e.g., Uber), or public transit	6.4
Paid a bill using your mobile phone's web browser or an app	18.7
Purchased a physical item or digital content remotely by using your mobile phone's web browser or an app	14.5
Made a donation or other payment using a text message	3.5
Number of respondents	2,244

Note: This question was asked of those with a mobile phone and includes those who did not identify themselves as having used mobile payments in the previous 12 months.

Table C.37. In the past month, about how many times have you used your mobile phone to make any type of mobile payment?

Q35 response	Percent, except as noted
Refused	0.8
Share of respondents with zero uses	25.5
Mean number of uses (at least one use)	4.1
Median number of uses (at least one use)	3.0
Number of respondents	436

Table C.38. In the past month, about how many times have you used your mobile phone to pay for a product or service at a store?

Q36 response	Percent, except as noted
Refused	1.8
Share of respondents with zero uses	25.3
Mean number of uses (at least one use)	3.7
Median number of uses (at least one use)	2.0
Number of respondents	192

Table C.39. You indicated that you have not made a mobile payment in a store in the past 12 months. Do you plan to use your mobile phone to make a payment in a store in the next 12 months?

Q34A response	Percent, except as noted
Refused	0.4
Definitely will use	3.6
Probably will use	12.0
Probably will not use	44.3
Definitely will not use	39.7
Number of respondents	2,045

Table C.40. When making mobile payments, which of the following payment methods do you use?

Q37 response	Percent, except as noted
Refused	1.8
Credit card	47.8
Debit card	56.4
Prepaid debit card	9.5
Bank account	36.1
Charge to your phone bill	3.3
Account at a non-financial institution (e.g., PayPal)	15.8
Other	1.9*
Number of respondents	436

* Fewer than 10 responses were received for this option.

Table C.41. When did you start using mobile payments?

Q38 response	Percent, except as noted
Refused	1.6
In the last 6 months	10.4
6 to 12 months ago	16.4
1 to 2 years ago	20.5
More than 2 years ago	30.4
I don't remember	20.8
Number of respondents	436

Table C.42. What was the main reason why you started using mobile payments when you did?

Q39 response	Percent, except as noted
Refused	2.7
I got a smartphone	20.4
The ability to make mobile payments became available	13.8
I became comfortable with the security of mobile payments	7.1
I liked the convenience of mobile payments	45.0
A store I visit started offering the service	2.5
To take advantage of loyalty or rewards points and discounts	4.0
Other	4.5
Number of respondents	436

Table C.43. Please tell us if each of the reasons below are why you do not use mobile banking.

Q40 response	Percent, except as noted
Refused/no to all	2.7
I'm concerned about the security of mobile banking	72.7
My banking needs are being met without mobile banking	87.9
I don't see any reason to use mobile banking	78.3
The mobile phone screen is too small	43.1
I don't have a smartphone	27.4
My bank charges a fee for using mobile banking	6.3
I don't do the banking in my household	15.3
I don't trust the technology	40.2
It's too difficult to use mobile banking	18.2
Number of respondents	819

Table C.44. Assuming that the concerns that you have about using mobile banking were addressed, would you be interested in doing any of the following activities with your mobile phone?

Q41 response	Percent, except as noted
Refused	1.1
Download your bank's mobile banking app	22.1
Check an account balance or recent transactions	35.2
Make bill payments using your bank's website or app	16.6
Receive alerts (e.g., text message, push notification, or e-mail) from your bank	25.1
Deposit a check electronically using a mobile phone camera	21.1
Transfer money between your bank accounts	18.6
Send money to relatives or friends within the U.S.	5.3
Send money to relatives or friends outside the U.S.	2.0
Locate the closest in-network ATM or branch	15.9
None, I don't want to use mobile banking	54.3
Number of respondents	819

Table C.45. If your bank or credit union were to offer mobile banking, would you be interested in doing any of the following activities with your mobile phone?

Q42 response	Percent, except as noted
Refused	1.2
Download your bank's mobile banking app	11.0
Check an account balance or recent transactions	17.4
Make bill payments using your bank's website or app	5.6
Receive alerts (e.g., text message, push notification, or e-mail) from your bank	7.3
Deposit a check electronically using a mobile phone camera	5.2
Transfer money between your bank accounts	5.1
Send money to relatives or friends within the U.S.	1.5*
Send money to relatives or friends outside the U.S.	0.1*
Locate the closest in-network ATM or branch	5.2
None, I don't want to use mobile banking	75.2
Number of respondents	536

* Fewer than 10 responses were received for this option.

Table C.46. Please tell us if any of the reasons below are why you do not use mobile payments.

Q43 response	Percent, except as noted
Refused/no to all	5.9
I'm concerned about the security of mobile payments	67.1
It's easier to pay with cash or a credit/debit card	80.0
I don't see any benefit from using mobile payments	64.9
The places I shop don't accept mobile payments	22.2
I don't have the necessary feature on my phone	36.1
I don't trust the technology	47.5
It's difficult or time consuming to set up or use mobile payments	34.3
I don't need to make any payments or someone else pays the bills	25.1
I don't really understand all the different mobile payment options	36.2
Number of respondents	1,802

Table C.47. Assuming that the reason(s) why you do not currently use mobile payments was addressed, would you be interested in doing any of the following activities with your mobile phone?

Q44 response	Percent, except as noted
Refused	1.0
Sending money to relatives or friends within the U.S.	5.8
Sending money to relatives or friends outside the U.S.	2.4
Paying for something in a store using your mobile phone/app instead of cash or a physical payment card	16.8
Paying for parking, a taxi, car service, or public transit	11.8
Paying a bill using your mobile phone's web browser or an app	11.7
Purchasing a physical item or digital content remotely by using your mobile phone's web browser or an app	11.7
Making a donation or other payment using a text message	4.8
None, I don't want to use mobile payments	74.2
Number of respondents	1,802

Table C.48. How safe do you believe people's personal information is when they use mobile banking?

Q45 response	Percent, except as noted
Refused	0.4
Very safe	7.8
Somewhat safe	35.2
Somewhat unsafe	24.3
Very unsafe	17.6
Don't know	14.7
Number of respondents	2,244

Table C.49. How safe do you believe people's personal information is when they use a mobile phone to pay for a purchase at a store?

Q46 response	Percent, except as noted
Refused	0.9
Very safe	6.4
Somewhat safe	32.1
Somewhat unsafe	26.6
Very unsafe	19.4
Don't know	14.7
Number of respondents	2,244

Table C.50. Which one of the following security aspects would cause you the most concern about using your mobile phone for financial transactions such as mobile banking or paying for a purchase in a store?

Q47 response	Percent, except as noted
Refused	0.4
My phone getting hacked or someone intercepting my data	25.1
Someone using my phone without permission to access my account	3.9
Losing my phone or having my phone stolen	13.4
Malware or viruses being installed on my phone	2.3
Companies misusing my personal information	1.9
Companies (merchants, banks, third parties) not providing sufficient security to protect my mobile transactions	7.3
All of the above	37.4
Other	0.8
No concerns/I think it is safe	7.7
Number of respondents	2,244

Table C.51. Do you already use, would like to use, or are unlikely to use your mobile phone for each of the following purposes?

Q48 response	Percent, except as noted			
	Refused	I already do	I would like to	I am unlikely to
Track your finances, purchases or expenses	1.0	33.4	13.8	51.9
Organize, track and store gift cards, memberships, loyalty and reward points	1.1	14.2	22.0	62.8
Compare prices when shopping	1.0	32.6	22.9	43.5
Receive and manage discount offers and coupons	1.1	25.5	24.9	48.5
Receive offers and promotions based on your location	1.0	18.9	22.3	57.8
Number of respondents	2,244			

Table C.52. I am willing to allow my mobile phone to provide my location to companies I shop with regularly so that they can offer me discounts, promotions, or services based on where I am.

Q49 response	Percent, except as noted
Refused	0.7
Strongly agree	5.7
Agree	34.7
Disagree	33.2
Strongly disagree	25.7
Number of respondents	1,680

Table C.53. I am willing to answer security questions or provide additional information to my bank or credit union when I log into mobile banking so that my bank can enhance the security of my mobile transaction.

Q50 response	Percent, except as noted
Refused	0.9
Strongly agree	31.8
Agree	42.0
Disagree	13.4
Strongly disagree	11.9
Number of respondents	1,680

Table C.54. Have you ever used your mobile phone to comparison shop over the Internet while at a retail store?

Q51 response	Percent, except as noted
Refused	0.9
Yes	44.9
No	54.1
Number of respondents	1,680

Table C.55. Have you ever used a barcode scanning app on your mobile phone while shopping at a retail store to find the best price for an item?

Q52 response	Percent, except as noted
Refused	0.6
Yes	28.2
No	71.2
Number of respondents	1,680

Table C.56. Has using your mobile phone to compare prices while you were shopping at a retail store ever changed where you made your purchase?

Q53 response	Percent, except as noted
Refused	0.1
Yes	69.0
No	30.9
Number of respondents	820

Table C.57. Have you ever scanned a QR code (similar to a barcode) in a retail store, newspaper, magazine, or billboard advertisement to obtain information about a product on your mobile phone?

Q54 response	Percent, except as noted
Refused	0.7
Yes	29.4
No	70.0
Number of respondents	1,680

Table C.58. Have you ever used your mobile phone to browse product reviews or get product information while shopping at a retail store?

Q55 response	Percent, except as noted
Refused	0.7
Yes	41.3
No	58.0
Number of respondents	1,680

Table C.59. Has reading product reviews on your mobile phone while shopping at a retail store ever changed which item you ended up purchasing?

Q56 response	Percent, except as noted
Refused	0.4
Yes	78.8
No	20.8
Number of respondents	662

Table C.60. In the past 12 months, have you used your mobile phone to check your account balance or available credit before making a large purchase?

Q57 response	Percent, except as noted
Refused	0.3
Yes	62.2
No	37.5
Number of respondents	775

Table C.61. Thinking of the most recent time that you checked your account balance or available credit before making a large purchase, did you decide not to buy that particular item because of the amount of money left in your account or the amount of your available credit?

Q58 response	Percent, except as noted
Refused	0.8
Yes	50.2
No	49.0
Number of respondents	444

Table C.62. Do you receive each of the following kinds of alerts?

Q59 response	Percent, except as noted
Refused	1.5
Low balance	46.0
Payment due	37.8
Saving reminders	6.5
Fraud	34.6
Credit card balance	19.2
Deposit or withdrawal	39.2
Statement available notification	38.8
Other	7.0
Number of respondents	594

Table C.63. Thinking of the most recent low-balance alert you received, which of the following actions did you take after receiving the alert?

Q60 response	Percent, except as noted
Refused	0.4
Transferred money into the account with the low balance from another account	42.9
Deposited money into the account with the low balance	35.5
Reduced my spending	29.9
None of the above	21.3
Number of respondents	256

Summary Statistics for Demographic Characteristics

Table C.64. Summary statistics for demographic characteristics: Full sample

Demographic characteristics	Weighted		Unweighted	
	Mean	Standard deviation	Mean	Standard deviation
Age	47.2005	17.2817	52.5630	16.7876
Male	0.4819	0.4998	0.5163	0.4998
Female	0.5181	0.4998	0.4837	0.4998
18–29	0.2133	0.4097	0.1227	0.3282
30–44	0.2513	0.4339	0.2012	0.4010
45–59	0.2657	0.4418	0.2956	0.4564
60+	0.2697	0.4439	0.3805	0.4856
Less than high school	0.1228	0.3283	0.0618	0.2408
High school degree	0.2959	0.4565	0.2633	0.4405
Some college	0.2831	0.4506	0.3040	0.4601
Bachelor's degree or higher	0.2982	0.4576	0.3709	0.4831
White, non-Hispanic	0.6489	0.4774	0.7645	0.4244
Black, non-Hispanic	0.1168	0.3213	0.0781	0.2684
Other, non-Hispanic	0.0793	0.2703	0.0637	0.2443
Hispanic	0.1549	0.3619	0.0936	0.2914
2+ races, non-Hispanic	0.0124	0.1109	0.0259	0.1589
Less than $25,000	0.1687	0.3746	0.1135	0.3173
$25,000–$39,999	0.2018	0.4014	0.1865	0.3896
$40,000–$74,999	0.1651	0.3713	0.1637	0.3701
$75,000–$99,999	0.2327	0.4226	0.2566	0.4368
Greater than $100,000	0.2317	0.4220	0.2797	0.4489
Married	0.5041	0.5001	0.6016	0.4897
Not married	0.4959	0.5001	0.3984	0.4897
Metropolitan	0.8488	0.3583	0.8570	0.3502
Northeast	0.1808	0.3849	0.1853	0.3886
Midwest	0.2132	0.4096	0.2283	0.4198
South	0.3717	0.4834	0.3578	0.4794
West	0.2343	0.4236	0.2287	0.4201
Employed	0.5829	0.4932	0.5526	0.4973
Unemployed, in labor force	0.0631	0.2432	0.0474	0.2126
Not in labor force	0.3540	0.4783	0.4000	0.4900
Observations	2,510			

Table C.65. Summary statistics for demographic characteristics: All mobile phone users (feature and smartphone)

Demographic characteristics	Weighted		Unweighted	
	Mean	Standard deviation	Mean	Standard deviation
Age	46.4496	16.9932	51.9020	16.5833
Male	0.4727	0.4994	0.5107	0.5000
Female	0.5273	0.4994	0.4893	0.5000
18–29	0.2212	0.4151	0.1270	0.3331
30–44	0.2578	0.4375	0.2077	0.4057
45–59	0.2706	0.4444	0.3004	0.4585
60+	0.2504	0.4334	0.3650	0.4815
Less than high school	0.1102	0.3132	0.0539	0.2259
High school degree	0.2827	0.4504	0.2536	0.4351
Some college	0.2921	0.4548	0.3093	0.4623
Bachelor's degree or higher	0.3150	0.4646	0.3832	0.4863
White, non-Hispanic	0.6513	0.4766	0.7660	0.4234
Black, non-Hispanic	0.1107	0.3139	0.0740	0.2618
Other, non-Hispanic	0.0793	0.2702	0.0642	0.2451
Hispanic	0.1587	0.3654	0.0958	0.2944
2+ races, non-Hispanic	0.0121	0.1093	0.0258	0.1587
Less than $25,000	0.1462	0.3534	0.0980	0.2974
$25,000–$39,999	0.1983	0.3988	0.1791	0.3836
$40,000–$74,999	0.1628	0.3693	0.1622	0.3687
$75,000–$99,999	0.2374	0.4256	0.2620	0.4398
Greater than $100,000	0.2552	0.4361	0.2986	0.4577
Married	0.5143	0.4999	0.6119	0.4874
Not married	0.4857	0.4999	0.3881	0.4874
Metropolitan	0.8599	0.3472	0.8632	0.3437
Northeast	0.1762	0.3810	0.1778	0.3824
Midwest	0.2137	0.4100	0.2277	0.4195
South	0.3654	0.4816	0.3619	0.4806
West	0.2448	0.4301	0.2326	0.4226
Employed	0.6119	0.4874	0.5740	0.4946
Unemployed, in labor force	0.0620	0.2412	0.0459	0.2093
Not in labor force	0.3261	0.4689	0.3801	0.4855
Observations	2,244			

Table C.66. Summary statistics for demographic characteristics: Smartphone users

Demographic characteristics	Weighted		Unweighted	
	Mean	Standard deviation	Mean	Standard deviation
Age	43.1405	15.8533	48.6601	15.9603
Male	0.4712	0.4993	0.5054	0.5001
Female	0.5288	0.4993	0.4946	0.5001
18–29	0.2640	0.4409	0.1565	0.3635
30–44	0.2973	0.4572	0.2464	0.4311
45–59	0.2553	0.4361	0.3113	0.4632
60+	0.1834	0.3871	0.2857	0.4519
Less than high school	0.0791	0.2700	0.0375	0.1900
High school degree	0.2742	0.4462	0.2369	0.4253
Some college	0.3030	0.4597	0.3167	0.4653
Bachelor's degree or higher	0.3437	0.4751	0.4089	0.4918
White, non-Hispanic	0.6294	0.4831	0.7440	0.4365
Black, non-Hispanic	0.1101	0.3130	0.0780	0.2682
Other, non-Hispanic	0.0898	0.2860	0.0714	0.2576
Hispanic	0.1707	0.3764	0.1065	0.3086
2+ races, non-Hispanic	0.0124	0.1108	0.0274	0.1632
Less than $25,000	0.1103	0.3134	0.0738	0.2615
$25,000–$39,999	0.1705	0.3762	0.1488	0.3560
$40,000–$74,999	0.1682	0.3742	0.1565	0.3635
$75,000–$99,999	0.2636	0.4407	0.2839	0.4510
Greater than $100,000	0.2873	0.4527	0.3369	0.4728
Married	0.5205	0.4997	0.6149	0.4868
Not married	0.4795	0.4997	0.3851	0.4868
Metropolitan	0.8800	0.3251	0.8780	0.3274
Northeast	0.1737	0.3790	0.1690	0.3749
Midwest	0.2024	0.4019	0.2185	0.4133
South	0.3636	0.4812	0.3720	0.4835
West	0.2603	0.4389	0.2405	0.4275
Employed	0.6876	0.4636	0.6530	0.4762
Unemployed, in labor force	0.0656	0.2477	0.0500	0.2180
Not in labor force	0.2468	0.4313	0.2970	0.4571
Observations	1,680			

Table C.67. Summary statistics for demographic characteristics: Feature phone users

Demographic characteristics	Weighted		Unweighted	
	Mean	Standard deviation	Mean	Standard deviation
Age	57.1376	16.0644	61.5342	14.5549
Male	0.4763	0.4999	0.5252	0.4998
Female	0.5237	0.4999	0.4748	0.4998
18–29	0.0822	0.2749	0.0396	0.1951
30–44	0.1302	0.3368	0.0935	0.2914
45–59	0.3187	0.4664	0.2644	0.4414
60+	0.4689	0.4995	0.6025	0.4898
Less than high school	0.2141	0.4105	0.1043	0.3059
High school degree	0.3063	0.4614	0.3022	0.4596
Some college	0.2582	0.4380	0.2860	0.4523
Bachelor's degree or higher	0.2214	0.4156	0.3076	0.4619
White, non-Hispanic	0.7198	0.4495	0.8291	0.3767
Black, non-Hispanic	0.1143	0.3184	0.0629	0.2431
Other, non-Hispanic	0.0452	0.2080	0.0432	0.2034
Hispanic	0.1207	0.3260	0.0647	0.2463
2+ races, non-Hispanic	0.0112	0.1053	0.0216	0.1454
Less than $25,000	0.2632	0.4407	0.1691	0.3751
$25,000–$39,999	0.2871	0.4528	0.2680	0.4433
$40,000–$74,999	0.1469	0.3543	0.1817	0.3859
$75,000–$99,999	0.1530	0.3603	0.1978	0.3987
Greater than $100,000	0.1498	0.3572	0.1835	0.3874
Married	0.4941	0.5004	0.6025	0.4898
Not married	0.5059	0.5004	0.3975	0.4898
Metropolitan	0.7948	0.4042	0.8201	0.3844
Northeast	0.1827	0.3868	0.2014	0.4014
Midwest	0.2494	0.4330	0.2554	0.4365
South	0.3748	0.4845	0.3345	0.4723
West	0.1931	0.3951	0.2086	0.4067
Employed	0.3630	0.4813	0.3345	0.4723
Unemployed, in labor force	0.0507	0.2197	0.0342	0.1818
Not in labor force	0.5863	0.4929	0.6313	0.4829
Observations	556			

Cross-Tabulations for Consumers' Use of Mobile Phones

Table C.68. Do you own or have regular access to a mobile phone?
Percent, except as noted

Age categories	No	Yes	Total	Number of respondents	Percentage of users in category
18–29	9.3	90.7	100.0	308	22.1
30–44	10.3	89.7	100.0	505	25.8
45–59	10.9	89.1	100.0	742	27.1
60+	18.8	81.2	100.0	955	25.0
Number of respondents	266	2,244	–	2,510	100.0

Table C.69. Is your mobile phone a smartphone?
Percent, except as noted

Age categories	Refused	No	Yes	Total	Number of respondents	Percentage of users in category
18–29	0.0	8.6	91.4	100.0	285	26.4
30–44	0.0	11.7	88.3	100.0	466	29.7
45–59	0.5	27.3	72.2	100.0	674	25.5
60+	0.5	43.4	56.1	100.0	819	18.3
Number of respondents	8	556	1,680	–	2,244	100.0

Table C.70. Do you own or have regular access to a mobile phone?
Percent, except as noted

Race/ethnicity	No	Yes	Total	Number of respondents	Percentage of users in category
White, non-Hispanic	12.2	87.8	100.0	1,919	65.1
Black, non-Hispanic	17.1	82.9	100.0	196	11.1
Other, non-Hispanic	12.2	87.8	100.0	95	6.7
Hispanic	10.5	89.5	100.0	235	15.9
2+ races, non-Hispanic	15.0	85.0	100.0	65	1.2
Number of respondents	266	2,244	–	2,510	100.0

Table C.71. Is your mobile phone a smartphone?
Percent, except as noted

Race/ethnicity	Refused	No	Yes	Total	Number of respondents	Percentage of users in category
White, non-Hispanic	0.4	25.6	74.0	100.0	1,719	62.9
Black, non-Hispanic	0.0	23.9	76.1	100.0	166	11.0
Other, non-Hispanic	0.0	11.7	88.3	100.0	86	7.7
Hispanic	0.0	17.6	82.4	100.0	215	17.1
2+ races, non-Hispanic	0.0	21.4	78.6	100.0	58	1.2
Number of respondents	8	556	1,680	–	2,244	100.0

Table C.72. Do you own or have regular access to a mobile phone?
Percent, except as noted

Gender	No	Yes	Total	Number of respondents	Percentage of users in category
Female	11.0	89.0	100.0	1,214	52.7
Male	14.2	85.8	100.0	1,296	47.3
Number of respondents	266	2,244	–	2,510	100.0

Table C.73. Is your mobile phone a smartphone?
Percent, except as noted

Gender	Refused	No	Yes	Total	Number of respondents	Percentage of users in category
Female	0.2	23	76.8	100.0	1,098	52.9
Male	0.3	23.4	76.3	100.0	1,146	47.1
Number of respondents	8	556	1,680	–	2,244	100.0

Table C.74. Do you own or have regular access to a mobile phone?
Percent, except as noted

Education	No	Yes	Total	Number of respondents	Percentage of users in category
Less than high school	21.6	78.4	100.0	155	11.0
High school	16.5	83.5	100.0	661	28.3
Some college	9.8	90.2	100.0	763	29.2
Bachelor's degree or higher	7.7	92.3	100.0	931	31.5
Number of respondents	266	2,244	–	2,510	100.0

Table C.75. Is your mobile phone a smartphone?
Percent, except as noted

Education	Refused	No	Yes	Total	Number of respondents	Percentage of users in category
Less than high school	0.0	45.0	55.0	100.0	121	7.9
High school	0.6	25.1	74.2	100.0	569	27.4
Some college	0.1	20.5	79.4	100.0	694	30.3
Bachelor's degree or higher	0.2	16.3	83.5	100.0	860	34.4
Number of respondents	8	556	1,680	–	2,244	100.0

Table C.76. Do you own or have regular access to a mobile phone?
Percent, except as noted

Income group	No	Yes	Total	Number of respondents	Percentage of users in category
Less than $25,000	24.2	75.8	100.0	285	14.6
$25,000–$39,999	14.1	85.9	100.0	468	19.8
$40,000–$74,999	13.8	86.2	100.0	411	16.3
$75,000–$99,999	10.8	89.2	100.0	644	23.7
Greater than $100,000	3.7	96.3	100.0	702	25.5
Number of respondents	266	2,244	–	2,510	100.0

Table C.77. Is your mobile phone a smartphone?
Percent, except as noted

Income group	Refused	No	Yes	Total	Number of respondents	Percentage of users in category
Less than $25,000	0.5	41.7	57.8	100.0	220	11.0
$25,000–$39,999	0.6	33.5	65.8	100.0	402	17.1
$40,000–$74,999	0.0	20.9	79.1	100.0	364	16.8
$75,000–$99,999	0.0	14.9	85.0	100.0	588	26.4
Greater than $100,000	0.2	13.6	86.2	100.0	670	28.7
Number of respondents	8	556	1,680	–	2,244	100.0

Cross-Tabulations for Consumers' Use of Mobile Banking and Mobile Payments

C.78.a. Cross-tabulations for consumers' use of mobile banking by age, race, gender, education, and income: Smartphone users
Percent, except as noted

Use of mobile banking in past 12 months	Refused	No	Yes	Total	Number of respondents	Percentage of users in category
Age categories						
18–29	0.0	30.3	69.7	100.0	240	33.2
30–44	0.7	36.3	63.0	100.0	392	34.9
45–59	0.0	56.8	43.2	100.0	512	21.4
60+	0.9	70.0	29.1	100.0	478	10.6
Number of respondents	4	843	775	–	1,622	100.0
Race/ethnicity						
White, non-Hispanic	0.3	51.4	48.3	100.0	1,218	58.4
Black, non-Hispanic	0.8	41.5	57.8	100.0	122	11.4
Other, non-Hispanic	0.0	41.3	58.7	100.0	72	8.8
Hispanic	0.9	33.6	65.5	100.0	168	20.3
2+ races, non-Hispanic	0.0	51.5	48.5	100.0	42	1.0
Number of respondents	4	843	775	–	1,622	100.0
Gender						
Female	0.4	46.3	53.3	100.0	801	53.2
Male	0.4	47.1	52.6	100.0	821	46.8
Number of respondents	4	843	775	–	1,622	100.0
Education						
Less than high school	3.9	45.3	50.8	100.0	49	6.1
High school	0.0	54.2	45.8	100.0	375	23.0
Some college	0.0	42.6	57.4	100.0	518	33.9
Bachelor's degree or higher	0.4	44.8	54.8	100.0	680	37.1
Number of respondents	4	843	775	–	1,622	100.0
Income group						
Less than $25,000	2.7	35.2	62.1	100.0	104	10.7
$25,000–$39,999	0.0	48.7	51.3	100.0	234	16.1
$40,000–$74,999	0.4	54.0	45.6	100.0	252	14.3
$75,000–$99,999	0.0	45.2	54.8	100.0	474	28.6
Greater than $100,000	0.3	46.2	53.5	100.0	558	30.3
Number of respondents	4	843	775	–	1,622	100.0

C.78.b. Cross-tabulations for consumers' use of mobile payments by age, race, gender, education, and income: Smartphone users
Percent, except as noted

Use of mobile payments in past 12 months	Refused	No	Yes	Total	Number of respondents	Percentage of users in category
Age categories						
18–29	0.9	66.9	32.2	100.0	263	30.1
30–44	0.5	63.3	36.2	100.0	414	38.1
45–59	0.0	77.2	22.8	100.0	523	20.6
60+	0.1	82.6	17.3	100.0	480	11.2
Number of respondents	6	1,268	406	–	1,680	100.0
Race/ethnicity						
White, non-Hispanic	0.4	76.5	23.1	100.0	1,250	51.4
Black, non-Hispanic	0.0	62.8	37.2	100.0	131	14.5
Other, non-Hispanic	0.0	56.0	44.0	100.0	74	12.0
Hispanic	0.8	65.0	34.2	100.0	179	20.6
2+ races, non-Hispanic	0.0	66.3	33.7	100.0	46	1.5
Number of respondents	6	1,268	406	–	1,680	100.0
Gender						
Female	0.5	70.2	29.3	100.0	831	54.8
Male	0.3	72.6	27.1	100.0	849	45.2
Number of respondents	6	1,268	406	–	1,680	100.0
Education						
Less than high school	0.0	69.6	30.4	100.0	63	8.5
High school	0.5	73.9	25.6	100.0	398	24.8
Some college	0.2	72.0	27.8	100.0	532	29.7
Bachelor's degree or higher	0.5	69.1	30.4	100.0	687	37.0
Number of respondents	6	1,268	406	–	1,680	100.0
Income group						
Less than $25,000	0.0	59.1	40.9	100.0	124	15.9
$25,000–$39,999	0.1	70.7	29.2	100.0	250	17.6
$40,000–$74,999	1.1	79.6	19.2	100.0	263	11.4
$75,000–$99,999	0.7	72.2	27.1	100.0	477	25.2
Greater than $100,000	0.0	70.7	29.3	100.0	566	29.7
Number of respondents	6	1,268	406	–	1,680	100.0

www.ingramcontent.com/pod-product-compliance
Lightning Source LLC
Chambersburg PA
CBHW080721190526
45169CB00006B/2461